The Day
the Markets
Roared

Also by Henry Kaufman

Interest Rates, the Markets, and the New Financial World

On Money and Markets: A Wall Street Memoir

The Road to Financial Reformation:
Warnings, Consequences, Reforms

Tectonic Shifts in Financial Markets:
People, Policies, and Institutions

The Day the Markets Roared

HOW A 1982 FORECAST SPARKED A GLOBAL BULL MARKET

HENRY KAUFMAN
with David B. Sicilia

Matt Holt Books
An Imprint of BenBella Books, Inc.
Dallas, TX

BenBella Books, Inc.
10440 N. Central Expressway
Suite 800
Dallas, TX 75231
www.benbellabooks.com
Send feedback to feedback@benbellabooks.com

BenBella is a federally registered trademark.
Matt Holt and logo are trademarks of BenBella Books.

Printed in the United States of America
10 9 8 7 6 5 4 3 2 1

Library of Congress Cataloging-in-Publication Data:
Names: Kaufman, Henry, author. | Sicilia, David B., author.
Title: The day the markets roared : how a 1982 forecast sparked a global bull market / Henry Kaufman, with David B. Sicilia.
Description: Dallas, TX : Matt Holt Books, [2021] | Includes bibliographical references and index. | Summary: "This book tells the story of a record day on Wall Street in mid-1982, the only time in post-war history when a private individual caused a bull market of such magnitude, exploring the global press reaction that followed, the backstory of Henry Kaufman's influence, and the lessons of that episode for today"—Provided by publisher.
Identifiers: LCCN 2020045344 (print) | LCCN 2020045345 (ebook) | ISBN 9781953295088 (hardback) | ISBN 9781953295200 (ebook)
Subjects: LCSH: Great Bull Market, 1982-1999. | Stock exchanges--United States--History--20th century. | Bull markets--United States--History--20th century. | Finance--Forecasting--History--20th century. | Capital market--History--20th century.
Classification: LCC HG4910 .K38 2021 (print) | LCC HG4910 (ebook) | DDC 332.64/27309048--dc23
LC record available at https://lccn.loc.gov/2020045344
LC ebook record available at https://lccn.loc.gov/2020045345

Copyediting by James Fraleigh
Proofreading by Jenny Bridges and
    Greg Teague
Indexing by WordCo Indexing Services
Text design and composition by Aaron
    Edmiston
Cover design by Sarah Avinger
Cover photo © Getty / Allan Tannenbaum
Printed by Lake Book Manufacturing

Distributed to the trade by Two Rivers Distribution, an Ingram brand
www.tworiversdistribution.com

Special discounts for bulk sales are available. Please contact bulkorders@benbellabooks.com.

To the memory of

William R. "Billy" Salomon

CONTENTS

Preface and Acknowledgments   ix
Introduction: August 17, 1982, in Context   1

PART I: WHAT HAPPENED

Chapter 1   The Day   11
Chapter 2   The Press Reaction   35

PART II: WHY IT HAPPENED

Chapter 3   Intellectual Roots   59
Chapter 4   Why I Was Bearish for So Long   71
Chapter 5   Albert M. Wojnilower, "Dr. Death"   93
Chapter 6   Critics, Threats, and Humor   107
Chapter 7   Growing Pressures   121

PART III: THE AFTERMATH

Chapter 8   Other Record Days on Wall Street   137
Chapter 9   Lessons   145
Chapter 10   New Realities   155

Bibliography   171
Notes   177
Index   187
About the Author   203

PREFACE AND ACKNOWLEDGMENTS

The genesis of this book occurred when Helen Katcher, my long-time assistant, walked into my office to tell me we were running out of filing space and she needed my help pruning some of the records we had accumulated over several decades. These records included a four-foot-wide set of large black leather-bound scrapbooks. Each thick album contained copies of my press interviews with US and foreign newspaper and magazine journalists, along with my shorter articles and editorials, printouts of television and radio interviews, and clippings of press reports that had quoted me over the years. During my years at Salomon Brothers (1962–1988), the company's public relations firm had collected and forwarded these materials to Ms. Katcher, who assembled them in the books. After I left Salomon, she continued to collect materials in the black volumes. There is one volume for each year.

Except for 1982, which took up two volumes. In fact, one of the two 1982 volumes is filled with press reports and other print media from a just a few days in the middle of August 1982—the subject of this book.

I had devoted a few paragraphs in one of my earlier books, *On Money and Markets* (2000), to my role in causing that bull market. Now, skimming through the 1982 volumes, it seemed I had given the topic—which business and economic historians have since portrayed as a milestone in financial history—short shrift.

I called David Sicilia, my editor for three of my previous books, to explore the idea of a book about August 17, 1982. He agreed that a narrative about a record-breaking day on Wall Street would make for a great story, but as a financial historian, he reminded me that readers also would need to understand the years-long backdrop to that historic day, as well as its aftermath, to fully grasp its causes and significance. What he was really telling me, I realized, was that the story of "the day the markets roared" (a title that came to me simultaneously with the book idea itself) needed to be situated in historical context. It was clear to me that to bring this book to fruition, I should write it in collaboration with David. And, indeed, his strong academic background as an associate professor of business, economic, and financial history at the University of Maryland proved to be extremely helpful in putting the events of mid-August 1982 in a proper perspective.

For the support she has given throughout my career, including her gracious assistance with this book and all my previous ones, I will be forever grateful to Helen Katcher. I also want to thank Peter Rup, a colleague of long standing, for supplying some of the statistical information for this book; Leah Spiro, my indefatigable book agent; and Matt Holt and his terrific team of editors and designers at Matt Holt Books for their fine work and commitment to the project.

Henry Kaufman
Franklin Lakes,
New Jersey

INTRODUCTION

AUGUST 17, 1982, IN CONTEXT

This book is about a record day on Wall Street—August 17, 1982. On that day, the stock market posted one of its largest single-day gains of the post–World War II period, and bond markets also rallied sharply. Interest rates were the driver—not in how they changed on that day, but in what I predicted about their long-term (secular) trend.

What happened on that single day was unique and a long time in the making. It was unique because it was the only time since the days of J. Pierpont Morgan when a forecast or any other action by a private individual caused a record-setting single-day rally (see chapter eight). It was a long time in the making because my reputation as an interest rate "guru," Salomon Brothers' position as the world's leading bond trader, and the postwar growth of the United States as a financial powerhouse all unfolded over decades. Accordingly, after describing what happened that fateful day (and its immediate aftermath) in the summer of 1982, this book looks back two decades to uncover the deep origins of the day the markets roared.

On record stock- or bond-trading days on the New York Stock Exchange, the Chicago Board of Trade, or elsewhere, no bell sounds on the floor to announce the achievement. Nor do the chair of the US Federal Reserve, the chair of the president's Council of Economic Advisers, or the US secretary of the Treasury announce such benchmarks. Nevertheless, financial market participants and many others throughout the wider economy are keenly interested to know the direction of the market, and record days often signal unique and important developments.

Major movements in stock prices influence business and household spending. Economist Paul Samuelson quipped about the impact of stock prices on business activity when he famously said, "The stock market has forecast nine out of the last five recessions." I suspect he might modify that view if he were around today to see how closely businesses and households monitor movements in both stock prices and interest rates. During Alan Greenspan's long tenure as chairman of the Federal Reserve, when he held chief responsibility for controlling interest rates, he also paid close attention to Wall Street, sometimes causing market movements with his pronouncements. His famous remark on December 5, 1996, when he speculated that "irrational exuberance has unduly escalated asset values," roiled markets worldwide. As a bull market nevertheless continued to rage during his tenure, Greenspan remained reluctant to take steps or even issue any more signals that might interrupt the Wall Street boom. He and many others understood the "wealth effect"—the fact that householders spend more liberally when they see the values of their investment portfolios or homes rising.

Along with stock prices, interest rates are also a major economic indicator and driver. They exercise immense influence over the availability of credit to all borrowers—households, businesses, and governments alike. Changes in interest rates affect the degree of risk taking by individual and institutional investors and can cause them to change the structures of their portfolios.

Stock prices, bond prices, and interest rates act on one another in generally predictable ways. Usually, but not always, stock prices and bond prices move in opposite directions. Usually, but not always, interest rates and bond prices also move in opposite directions. Predicting the exact degree of these movements is a more difficult challenge.

The United States established a robust financial sector soon after its birth as a nation. Whereas leading general merchants had provided a variety of financial services during the colonial period—private and commercial lending, insurance underwriting, international trade, among others—the economy of the early national period grew enough to support financial specialization. The first free-standing insurance companies and banks appeared in the late 1700s and early 1800s, as semi-organized clusters of securities traders appeared on the southern tip of Manhattan—the first "curbstone brokers" prefiguring the great exchanges to come.

In the nineteenth century, the financial sector grew to meet the demands of early industrialization, the growth of slavery, and internal improvements such as canals, railroads, and telegraphs. Late in the century, with the rise of big business, a robust market for industrial securities emerged. A new breed of powerful investment bankers—none more powerful than the House of Morgan—dominated the age of "finance capitalism" as they reorganized railroads, forged giant industrial combines like United States Steel and International Harvester, and periodically rescued the federal government from bankruptcy. The establishment of the Federal Reserve in 1913 brought a degree of stability to the system, but met its match with the twin economic calamities of the Wall Street Crash of 1929 and the Great Depression.

It wasn't until after World War II that America's rapidly growing middle class began to participate widely in the financial sector; before then, stock and bond investing and ready access to credit were prerogatives of the wealthy. Now, federal programs to encourage home ownership fueled a massive postwar residential construction boom. Credit cards became commonplace. Discount brokerage firms aimed at middle-class households appeared. Branch banking and (later) ATMs proliferated. American multinational corporations spread rapidly around the world. The federal government borrowed and invested heavily in interstate highway building, national defense, and social welfare programs. The United States enjoyed the greatest economic expansion in human history, and with it came a surge in financial wealth. Americans—more and more of them college educated—became literate in basic economic and financial matters, following them with great interest in daily newspapers and on television.

By the early 1980s, when the core events described in this book took place, the United States had entered a new era that later was labeled "financialization." Its hallmarks were

- an explosion in the variety and traded volume of marketable securities (such as derivatives, certificates of deposit, mortgage-backed securities, etc.);
- growing internationalization of financial activities, especially in the volume and velocity of securities and currency trading;

- the expansion of the financial sector as a percentage of the larger economy;
- the rising profitability of the financial sector;
- financial deregulation;
- the emergence of diversified financial conglomerates engaged in multiple activities (such as commercial banking, investment banking, credit card issuance, money management, and insurance);
- the concentration of financial assets and business into a shrinking number of giant firms
- the rise of econometric risk modeling in finance; and
- a growing culture of financial risk taking in response to competitive pressures.

We can only understand the events of mid-August 1982 within that historical context. Interest rates continued to be one of the most important indicators and determinants of economic performance. Stock trading kept attracting more attention than the bond market, but the latter was (and remains) several times larger than equities markets (in value of assets). Interest rates were therefore a more reliable gauge of economic health.

Indeed, interest rates played an even more prominent role in the economy of the time than during earlier periods of US history, partly thanks to financialization. As figure I.1 illustrates, throughout the nineteenth and the first half of the twentieth centuries, long-term bond rates had moved in a range of 2.5 to 8.0 percent. Long-term, or "secular," swings were sometimes difficult to identify.

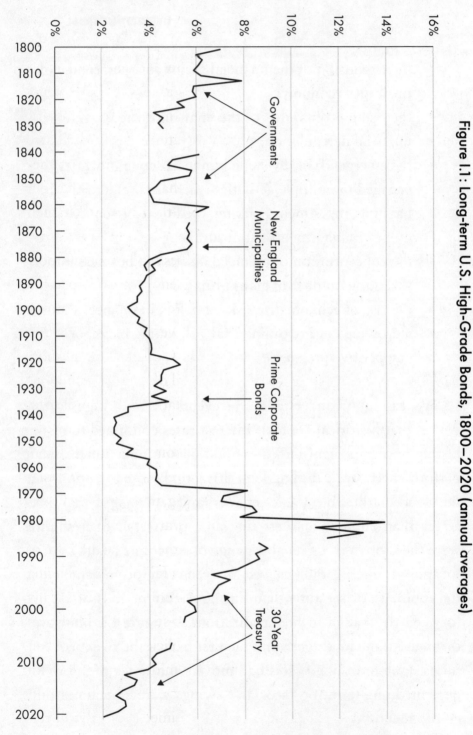

Figure I.1: Long-term U.S. High-Grade Bonds, 1800–2020 (annual averages)

Since the Second World War, bond interest rates have risen and fallen in a long secular cycle. (Courtesy Collection of Henry Kaufman)

The post–World War II period was different. The yield on US government bonds rose steeply, with only a handful of interruptions, from its historic low of 2.5 percent in 1945 to its historic high of 15.25 percent in October 1981. (Interest yields vacillated for a few years after that but, as we can now see clearly, they had entered a long-term secular decline that has stretched four decades to the start of the 2020s, when they now sit at their all-time low in American history.)

This enormous secular cycle in US interest rates explains more than any other single fact why my 1982 memo was so impactful. In our current age of "big data," we speak of signals and noise. "Signals" are the big, important trends we look for—whether political polling trends, market movements, or meaningful shifts in crime statistics. "Noise" is the vast cloud of data—the millions or billions or trillions of data points—that potentially distract from the big picture.

By the early 1980s, investors and economic experts from Wall Street to Main Street were desperately looking for a signal, as they wondered, "When is it going to end?!" "It" was the relentless three-and-a-half-decade upward march of interest rates. The higher interest rates climbed, the higher the cost of borrowing money, doing business, building factories, and buying houses and cars. Inflation also had been running at historically high peacetime levels, despite the efforts of several Fed chairmen to bring it under control, although the policies of Paul Volcker (who became head of the central bank in mid-1979) were yielding results by the early 1980s.

My August 17, 1982, memo was not timed perfectly. In retrospect, we know that the secular reversal in interest rates after

World War II had occurred in October 1981. I hadn't caught the signal amid the noise, and I talk about why in a later chapter. Why, then, did my memo have such an enormous impact coming when it did? One major reason was that I had been bearish on interest rates for decades, while most economists and Wall Street forecasters were more bullish, but had been proven wrong again and again.

My memo did not forecast lower interest rates years into the future, nor did it declare a secular reversal. And it certainly didn't *cause* interest rates to reverse direction. But because of my reputation on Wall Street by that time, my routine observations made the news. When I changed my stance, it was major news. So changing my stance about one of the most pressing economic issues of the day—after holding out for decades—sparked a global reaction.

Part I

What Happened

Chapter 1

The Day

Tuesday, August 17, 1982, began partly cloudy and humid, even for a summer day in the Mid-Atlantic Region. But I paid little heed as I walked the few steps from the front door of my house in Wyckoff, New Jersey, to the waiting Lincoln Town Car at 6:30 AM. My driver, Timothy Mulally, was ready to take me into Manhattan for a meeting of the Salomon Brothers Executive Committee. As usual, I found crisp morning editions of the *Wall Street Journal* and the *New York Times* on the back seat.

After exchanging a few pleasantries with Tim, I eagerly plunged into the newspapers as we wound our way east through the suburbs on the hour-long drive into Manhattan. The morning papers would be a welcome distraction—not only from the inevitably gnarled traffic we typically confronted at that hour once we reached the George Washington Bridge—but on this day, they might take my mind off the memo I had been crafting for nearly a week. Except for some final proofreading, it was ready to go. But my mind was more focused on the 8:00 AM Executive Committee meeting.

I soon discovered on both newspapers' front pages several stories that immediately captured my interest, and virtually all of them held implications for national or international financial markets and economic relations. It was indeed an eventful time, with rapid change and instability adding to a general atmosphere of uncertainty. In retrospect, that uncertainty contributed to the powerful reaction that my memo would generate as the day unfolded.

On the international front, America had signed a new communiqué with China over arms manufacturing designed to ease US–Chinese tensions over Taiwan. The new agreement paved the way for Taiwan to eventually manufacture F5-E fighter jets independently of the American firm Northrop Corporation, but not more-advanced US military aircraft models. Still, much about the independence and international status of this emerging "Asian Tiger" remained uncertain. I had become increasingly interested in East Asian financial markets since 1976, when Salomon Brothers opened a small office in Hong Kong.

As a Jew, I was buoyed by the news that Philip Habib, the US special envoy to the Middle East, saw little left to resolve in the current round of Middle East peace negotiations, now that the Palestine Liberation Organization had agreed to withdraw its forces from west Beirut. In spite of numerous setbacks, hopes for lasting peace in the Middle East had improved dramatically in the past three and a half years since Egyptian president Anwar Sadat and Israeli prime minister Menachem Begin signed the Egypt–Israel Peace Treaty. Little did I or most of the rest of the world expect that fourteen months from that sultry August morning, Egyptian and Syrian forces would invade the Sinai Peninsula and the Golan Heights during Judaism's holiest holiday, Yom Kippur, touching off a war and an Arab oil embargo that would roil the global economy for many years.

As with these two stories, international developments almost always carried business and economic implications, and the same was true of the main report out of Latin America that morning. The Dominican Republic's new president, Salvador Jorge Bianco, made a startling declaration during his official inauguration speech: his country was "financially bankrupt." Bianco blamed the United States and Europe for his nation's economic travails—specifically, he complained, US tariffs and import quotas on Dominican sugar, and large US budget deficits, were keeping "international interest rates exaggeratedly high." According to the report, Bianco did not also lament the staggering debt crisis that had erupted in the region only a matter of weeks earlier, hitting Mexico and Argentina especially hard, thanks in large part to the reckless Latin American lending practices of Citibank under CEO Walter Wriston.

Wriston and I disagreed publicly and privately over his efforts to break down the long-standing barriers between different types of financial institutions; and indeed, more than any other executive in modern US financial history, Wriston was responsible for the rise of giant, highly diversified "financial supermarkets." As reported that August morning, Wriston had taken another step in that direction the previous day when the Federal Home Loan Bank Board gave preliminary approval to Citibank—then the nation's second-largest bank holding company—to expand its operations into California by purchasing a major savings and loan association, Fidelity Savings and Loan Association of San Francisco. The

Federal Reserve was expected to approve the move after September 4 hearings in California, making Citibank the first American bank permitted to establish an out-of-state deposit institution. The *Times* reported that state regulators, California banks, and the savings and loan industry "bitterly opposed" the move. Since I had been issuing warnings in speeches and articles about the mainly negative consequences of growing financial conglomeration, that morning's report of the likely Citibank–Fidelity deal was, for me, very unwelcome news.

As for the domestic economic scene, news during that period was seldom uplifting. What became known as the "Reagan Recession" had taken hold the previous summer, and the unemployment rate was now hovering around 7.5 percent. Much of this was the result of the yeoman's efforts of my friend and former colleague, Federal Reserve Chairman Paul Volcker, to wring long-damaging double-digit inflation out of the economy. That effort would pay off another year or so down the road, but in the meantime the economic pain was deep. General Motors was reported that morning to be shedding about 9,100 jobs by shuttering two factories and eliminating work shifts in others because of the "gloomy outlook" in the automobile market.

For their part, federal economic policymakers, from President Ronald Reagan and Congress on down, were struggling both to revive economic growth and to slow the growth of the budget deficit and national debt. Only a year and a half into the optimistic president's administration, it was becoming abundantly clear that his supply-side approach was yielding massive budgetary shortfalls. But politicians were taking action, according to that morning's news. Congressional conferees announced they had

agreed on an additional $13.6 billion in spending cuts that, com-
bined with other cuts and tax increases, were projected to reduce
the federal deficit by nearly $130 billion over the next three years.
And the previous evening, in a short but momentous address to
the nation, President Reagan had issued a bipartisan appeal to
Congress to *raise* taxes $98.3 billion over the next three fiscal
years—a speech the *Times* called "a significant change of theme
for his Administration." As columnist Howell Raines observed

Figure 1.1 By August 1982, Paul Volcker's tough but necessary Fed policies were beginning to
wring double-digit inflation out of the economy. (George Tames/The New York Times/Redux)

in a related front-page story, "with the economy still mired in a recession, Mr. Reagan has tilted back toward traditional Republican economics."

The president's reversal on taxes was the big domestic economic news that morning. But what held my attention more were reports that Treasury bill rates had fallen to their lowest level in about two years. Although most banks had cut their prime rates 50 basis points to 14.5 percent in response, Bankers Trust cut its fee to 14 percent and, according to the *Wall Street Journal*, "that level is expected to be widespread soon." The paper quoted John D. Paulus, the chief economist at Goldman Sachs (soon to move to Morgan Stanley), who stated that the popularity of Treasuries was a symptom of "worries about creditworthiness in troubled times" but also that rates were now "low enough to help turn the economy around." The *Journal* also quoted Albert M. Wojnilower, First Boston Corporation's chief economist, at some length. Wojnilower—whose career and previous day's analysis I discuss in chapter five—predicted that "both short- and long-term interest rates on top-quality obligations will be noticeably lower next year," but went on to caution that, given the current business climate, near-term rates would "remain vulnerable to an upward movement," as the *Journal* reported.

The forecast I now carried in my briefcase—generally similar to Wojnilower's but less equivocal and based on different analysis—would, by the end of that business day, prove to be explosive.

We were not headed for the Salomon Brothers office building in lower Manhattan, but rather toward the Waldorf-Astoria Hotel on Park Avenue in Midtown. Completed in 1931—the same year as another Art Deco Manhattan landmark, the Empire State Building, which was built on the site of the original (1893) Waldorf-Astoria—the "new" Waldorf had been the tallest hotel in the world until 1963, and remained one of the most luxurious, as well as an elite venue for many conferences and high-level diplomatic, political, business, and fundraising meetings. On this morning, beginning around 8:00 AM, the Salomon Brothers

Figure 1.2 In the early 1980s, the Salomon Brothers Executive Committee preferred to meet at the elegant Waldorf-Astoria Hotel, away from the company's hectic downtown headquarters. *(Photo by Edmund Vincent Gillon/Museum of the City of New York/Getty Images)*

Executive Committee would meet in a suite in the Towers portion of the hotel, away from the kinds of interruptions likely at the company headquarters at One New York Plaza. We entered the Towers not through the main Park Avenue entrance but through a private doorway around the corner.

As I climbed out of the car, I asked Tim to deliver a copy of my memo downtown to my secretary, Helen Katcher, with instructions for her to phone me after she had typed it (see Figure 1.3).

While it is difficult for me to generalize about the other seven members of the Executive Committee, to say they were extremely talented and aggressive about financial matters goes a long way. Richard Rosenthal headed the firm's equity arbitrage. He had left high school at age fifteen to become a runner at a small brokerage firm, and soon landed a job at L.F. Rothschild, where he excelled at trading convertible securities. Shrewd sometimes to the point of being cunning and devious, and lacking managerial skills, he joined Salomon in 1965, and was now the Executive Committee's youngest member.

J. Ira Harris joined Salomon in 1968 after building a reputation as a mergers and acquisitions master at Blair & Co. Deft at relationship building and negotiations, he continued to shine at Salomon by engineering, among many others, the $109 million merger of Walter E. Heller International with American National Bank & Trust. He headed the firm's Chicago office.

William Vouté had joined Salomon in 1960 and recently joined the Executive Committee. He was in charge of the firm's corporate and international bond trading. One of two non-Jews on the Committee (Richard Schmeelk was the other), he was active in the Roman Catholic Archdiocese of New York.

8/17/82

SPECIAL NOTICE

Following is a Memorandum to Portfolio Managers that will be mailed to clients
tonight.

THE PROSPECTS FOR INTEREST RATES

Recent events in the economy and financial markets require a new look at
the prospects for interest rates. On balance, these events suggest that the
decline in interest rates now underway will continue, irregular to be sure, with
perhaps dramatic interruptions. On balance, however, long-term U.S. Government
bonds, now yielding about 12 1/2%, may well fall into the 9% to 10% range sometime
within the next twelve months. The Federal funds rate, now 10%, may decline to
a low of 6 to 7%.

The immediate threat that would have driven long-term interest rates back
to their 1981 peak yields -- a smart business recovery in the second half of
this year -- is now much less likely to materialize than a few months ago.
Besides consumer spending that is holding at a high plateau (but is failing to
gain ground because of weaknesses elsewhere) and the rise in defense spending, the
remainder of the economy is straitjacketed by financial blockages and tough
international competition.

It will take considerable further declines in interest rates and time to
unwind major financial impediments to significant economic expansion. In particular,
the refurbishing of business balance sheets and profitability is now an overriding
priority of corporate management. This priority cannot be quickly reversed.
The corporate financial structure has become extremely fragile. Corporate debt
is top-heavy, resulting in credit quality deterioration. Profitability is under
great pressure. Capacity utilization in manufacturing is at an extremely low
69%. The efforts to reduce inventories is now being joined by massive cutbacks
in capital outlays. These measures will contribute to a stagnant economy, and to

Figure 1.3 This typed version of the memo went to portfolio managers
at Salomon Brothers. *(Courtesy Collection of Henry Kaufman)*

-2-

a sharp contraction in business external financing which as in the past will be
an important contributing factor to the fall in long-term interest rates.

Equally important, major financial institutions are in no position to carry
on aggressive lending and investing strategy that would propel the economy ahead
With a fall in interest rates, the initial response of thrifts will have to be to
to improve their liquidity and to minimize the risks in their long-term assets.
Moreover, no new boom in housing activity is likely. Variable interest rates have
reduced financing incentives to home buyers and housing costs remain very high.
Commercial bank strategy is limited by a thin capital base, and substantial
non-earning assets which may actually increase if the economy does not rebound
rapidly. Even insurance companies are forced to cope with cash flow and profitability
problems this time around of much greater magnitude than in the past.

Internationally, too, the massive debt overhang restricts the capacity of
financial institutions as a stimulative force. Economic stagnation both here and
abroad will continue to breed its own retarding forces. The continued strength
of the dollar as American interest rates have been coming down is also a sign
of considerable disequilibrium that will probably result in a highly competitive
environment for American goods and services in the international markets and more
credit problems.

The extent of the interruptions in the decline in interest rates in the
months ahead depends partly on the extent to which monetary policy reverts to the
enforcement of the monetarist approach. There is no way in telling when the
substantial infusion of new reserves will trigger money growth above official
targets just as it also may be difficult to tell at that time whether this spurt
in money supply will be due to technical factors or new underlying demands from
a growing economy. A prompt or a belated response by the Fed will temporarily push
the funds rate up again and will stall the funding of liabilities and the general

-3-

reliquefication needed to bring the economy out of its doldrums. A significant
narrowing of the sharply sloped positive yield curve through a significant lift
in short rates will interrupt, therefore, the rally in long bonds. However, it
is unlikely to terminate it because the reliquefication needs of the economy,
which are extremely large, will also be interrupted.

The huge budget deficit is another factor that will periodically interrupt
the bond rally. Signs of business recovery and large new U.S. issues will induce
investor cautiousness at times while the lack of business recovery will induce
investors to préfer U.S. Government obligations over private credit instruments.
Large Treasury deficits will also limit the ability of the Fed to follow a
consistently easier policy. For the foreseeable future, there will be a massive
supply of high quality U.S. Government while the credit quality of private
obligations will probably decline.

The problem in assessing the potential for the total interest rate decline
during the next year hinges importantly in determining the interest rate level that
will rejuvenate economic activity to a much higher level. In a conventional
cyclical setting, historical benchmarks were very helpful in this determination.
Now, the answer lies on the extent to which the credit structure has been
seriously impaired. Great impairment will require much larger than expected drops
in interest rates. In this connection, no clearcut estimate can be formulated.
The interest rate projections stated at the start of this memo should be
taken with this qualification in mind.

                                        Henry Kaufman

Gedale Horowitz, an attorney and graduate of Columbia Law School, oversaw the firm's municipal bond operations, having emerged as the Municipal Department's senior trader by 1964 at the age of thirty-two. Not one of the Committee's stronger personalities, he typically preferred to listen rather than debate.

Thomas Strauss, the managing director of government bonds, also held a graduate degree—in his case from the University of Pennsylvania. He and Gedale typified the younger breed of degree-holding Salomon executives who found themselves mixing with an earlier generation of streetwise rainmakers.

A prime example of the latter was Richard Schmeelk, the head of corporate finance. His career on Wall Street began humbly at Salomon in 1941, as a runner. He served in the Navy during World War II, then returned to the firm to observe and train in a variety of posts until he was assigned to the then-tiny Canadian commercial paper market. Affable and well liked, Schmeelk became known as "Mr. Canada" as he impressively built underwriting and sales north of the border. (He later endowed a generous scholarship fund for Canadian graduate students.) In 2019, the government of Canada awarded him with its highest honor for a foreigner, the Order of Canada.

Then there was the firm's managing partner, John Gutfreund. He had graduated from Oberlin College in 1951 with a degree in English, served two years in the US Army, then landed a trainee position at Salomon in the Statistical Department before migrating to the Municipal Department, then the Syndicate Department. William R. "Billy" Salomon, the son of one of the firm's founders (Percy), had been the firm's managing partner since 1963, and had skillfully moved the firm to the upper echelon of investment banking. Salomon chose Gutfreund to succeed him in 1978, but eventually came to regret the decision (see chapter four).

Soon after the meeting got underway, the conversation turned to some festering issues on everyone's minds related to Salomon Brothers' recent merger with the Phibro Corporation. Salomon had been attracted to Phibro mainly to gain access to its large capital holdings. The new holding company, Phibro-Salomon, was headed by Phibro's CEO, David Tendler. Beyond that, the new president, Hal Beretz, hailed from Phibro, as did most of the new firm's directors. Even though Salomon and Phibro were managed by separate subsidiaries under the holding company umbrella, overall management control lay predominantly with prior Phibro executives. Recently, however, the Salomon operation was resurging in profitability while the Phibro unit's business was flagging. It was a classic power struggle, and the men in the room—leaders of the holding company's Salomon subsidiary—wanted to regain more of it.

At around 8:15 AM the phone rang. One of my partners picked up the phone in the next room and said, "Henry, it's your secretary, Helen. She needs to talk to you." I told John that I needed to take the call. Somewhat annoyed, he told me to make it quick. Helen read the memo to me. I made a few corrections and told her to release the memo simultaneously to the press and internally to Salomon. It was a full ten or fifteen minutes before I returned to the meeting, by which time everyone seemed annoyed.

"What was all that about, and why keep us sitting here waiting?" John demanded.

I told the group that I had changed my view on the market and that a substantial additional interest-rate decline was coming.

There was a brief but weighty silence, with several looks of astonishment. Then came the questions. Ira Harris and Tom Strauss asked the most. What had I actually said? How had I made the announcement? I told the members that I had changed my forecast for interest rates. Specifically, I had announced that in the next twelve months long-term US government bonds would fall from 12.75 percent to 9 to 10 percent, and the Federal funds rate from 10 percent to 6 to 7 percent.

The general reaction was: *"What? You said that?"*

When John Gutfreund spoke, he began by pointing out that at Salomon's regular Monday sales and traders meeting the day before, I had not mentioned my changed position, then asked, "Why?" I reminded him and the others what everyone knew from long-standing practice: as head of the company's research departments, I always put important announcements in writing. Did that mean, others wanted to confirm, I had not discussed my new stance with any Salomon traders, salespeople, investment bankers, or even with my colleagues in research? And what about the firm's major clients, with whom I met regularly? To all these questions, I answered "no." Despite questions that would emerge within days, and even an official inquiry that came shortly thereafter, on this day as on previous days, Salomon Brothers learned about my analysis at the same time as our clients and the larger Wall Street community.

It was around this time that, in spite of our best efforts to avoid interruption, someone at the trading desk at One New York Plaza reached us by telephone. The bond market was rallying sharply, and even though the stock market had not yet opened, it was poised to open significantly higher.

John took another call soon after the market opened at 10:00 AM.* It was deluged with buy orders, and the bond market continued its rally. When he asked what was behind it all, the caller replied, "Henry's memo." We quickly adjourned the meeting and hurried downtown to Salomon headquarters.

One New York Plaza sits at the tip of Manhattan just across from Governor's Island and within view of the Statue of Liberty. In search of much greater space to meet its growing needs, Salomon had moved from 60 Wall Street into the sleek new glass-façade building in 1970. I rushed up to the forty-first floor, which housed our trading operations and research departments. The trading floor was based on the same concept as its predecessor at 60 Wall Street: bring together all the key trading and sales functions in close proximity so that market information could travel quickly. The old space was known as "the Financial Supermarket." The new one—where government securities traders worked alongside those trading in corporate and municipal bonds and notes, money market instruments, mortgage securities, and equities—was called "The Room." All of those specialists were in turn linked electronically with our regional offices and subsidiaries in the US, Europe, and the Far East.

This integration of activities was vital to the firm's success. Salomon's senior management recognized early on that developments in one sector of the financial markets often affected the price structure of other markets. For example, a very successful

---

* Since 1985, the NYSE opening bell has sounded at 9:30 am.

new offering of bonds by the US Treasury frequently influences the price of corporate bonds. In a bull market, bonds selling at a discount may rally more than bonds selling at a premium, affecting the price relationships in many markets.

Traders, salespeople, and partners involved in trading and sales occupied desks in The Room. So did the managing partner (then John Gutfreund), who always had a private office but spent much of his day presiding over the vast trading floor while seated at a desk on one side of the trading floor. There he would often huddle with key trading partners. Sometimes, for instance, they had to decide quickly whether to consummate a large trade in which Salomon Brothers would take a big portion of the trade into its inventory.

By the early 1980s, The Room had become iconic, a national and international symbol of the rough-and-tumble world of high finance. The traders—nearly all men back then—sat in pairs at cluttered U-shaped desks that ran end to end across the floor in long rows. Shedding their jackets in the crowded environment, they sported white shirts with rolled-up sleeves. Their essential tools were the computer terminal, the telephone, and their own ears and vocal cords—for a great deal of market information was gleaned from overheard phone conversations or shouted from one desk to another. This roiling culture of sound and (during heavy trading days) fury was popularized and memorialized in the decade's fiction and nonfiction. In Tom Wolfe's best-selling 1987 novel about the excesses of Wall Street high-fliers, *The Bonfire of the Vanities*, the main bond trading room of the fictionalized investment house "Pierce & Pierce" bears an eerie similarity to The Room at One New York Plaza, although here

Wolfe exercised poetic license by lowering the ceiling to enhance the sense of sweaty close-quarters work:

> It was a vast space, perhaps sixty by eighty feet, but with the same eight-foot ceiling bearing down on your head. It was an oppressive space with a ferocious glare, writhing silhouettes, and the roar. The glare came from a wall of plate glass that faced south, looking out over New York Harbor, the Statue of Liberty, Staten Island, and the Brooklyn and New Jersey shores. The writhing silhouettes were the arms and torsos of young men, few of them older than forty. They had their suit jackets off. They were moving about in an agitated manner and sweating early in the morning and shouting, which created the roar.

Figure 1.4 "The Room"—the vast Salomon Brothers trading floor—exemplified Wall Street in the 1980s and was imitated by other investment houses. *(Allan Tannenbaum/Getty Images)*

In *Liar's Poker*, Michael Lewis—a former Salomon salesman in New York and London before transforming himself into a best-selling business journalist (thanks to this book)—recalled The Room this way: "Most of the men were on two phones at once. Most of the men stared at small green screens full of numbers. They'd shout into one phone, then into the other, then at someone across the row of trading desks, then back into the phones, then point to the screen and scream, '*Fuck!*' Thirty seconds was considered a long attention span."

Over time, other investment houses emulated the Salomon approach to floor trading by building their own versions of our roiling arena at One New York Plaza. But for now we were the pioneers and (to borrow a phrase from Wolfe) the "Masters of the Universe" in bond trading.

When I entered The Room the morning of August 17, 1982, the roar was at record levels. The avalanche of orders easily overwhelmed our state-of-the-art communications equipment, which added to the need for cross-row shouting. Some of the traders and salespeople glanced up at me, the cause of all the uproar, and stared for a few seconds before returning to the fray. As I walked to my office, some of the partners and managers tried to grab a word with me or offered exclamations like "Look what's going on, Henry!" or "I've never seen such a day!"

At my office I was greeted by a long list of phone messages from clients and journalists in the US and abroad who were asking for interviews. On normal days, I fielded such requests myself, but on more momentous occasions I called on our Manhattan-based outside public relations firm, Adams & Rinehart, Inc. That day, the PR firm helped manage the flood of media requests. For the time being, we declined them all.

The rest of the day was a blur of cascading trade orders, market reports, and shattered records. From late-day and next-day market reports, we can reconstruct the day's movements with some precision.

It took only fifteen minutes after Treasury bonds traded on the Chicago Board of Trade to reach their daily limit of two points after trading there began at 9:00 AM. Stock trading similarly surged immediately after opening, so that by 10:19 the Dow Jones Industrial Average was up 5.90 points, with the ticker tape running two minutes behind. One minute later, Manufacturers Hanover Trust cut its prime rate from 14.5 percent to 14 percent. By 11:00, the Dow was up nearly 11 points. After retreating slightly, it hit 807.74 at 2:00 in the afternoon—a huge gain of 15.31 points. More bank rate cuts followed, with Bankers Trust announcing at 2:08 that it was slashing its broker-loan rate from 12.50 to 11.75 percent, followed by a reduction in Citibank's prime from 14.50 to 14.00 percent less than ninety minutes later.

When the closing bell sounded at 4:30, the Dow stood at 831.24, an increase of 38.81 points, or 4.90 percent. (To put this in present-day perspective, a 4.90 percent gain on a Dow of 30,000 would mean a one-day gain of 1,470 points.) Similarly, the Standard & Poor's Index, which had closed the previous day at 104.09, had gained nearly 5 points, for a 4.76 percent gain. Both were the largest single-day gains in Wall Street history up to that point. The Dow nearly set a daily volume record as well, with some 92,860,000 shares traded.

A Chronology: How The Stock Market Scored Record Rise

* * *

By a WALL STREET JOURNAL Staff Reporter

A chronology of events in the hectic U.S. financial markets yesterday:

9:15 a.m. (EDT): Treasury bonds for September delivery on the Chicago Board of Trade rally the daily limit of two points in the first 15 minutes of trading. Traders say Salomon Brothers' purchase of 1,200 bond contracts for futures delivery boosts the market.

9:40: Rumors that Salomon Brothers' chief economist, Henry Kaufman, sees long-term rates declining to the 9% to 10% range send bond prices surging as much as 2¼ points in hectic trading.

10:00: At the opening of trading, stocks are mostly above yesterday's closing prices.

10:19: The stock-quotation tape runs two minutes late; the Dow Jones Industrial Average is up 5.90 points.

10:20: Manufacturers Hanover Trust Co. of New York cuts its prime rate to 14% from 14½%. New York's Bankers Trust Co. and Cleveland's AmeriTrust Co. had cut their prime rates to 14% the previous day. Stocks rise sharply in heavy trading. The Dow Jones Industrial Average is up nearly five points.

10:41: Mr. Kaufman confirms he sees further decline in rates.

11:10: Stocks move sharply higher on growing expectations of rate declines. The Industrial Average is up almost 9 points.

12:38 p.m. The Industrial Average is up about 8 points after having a 10-point rise earlier.

2:00: The Industrial Average is up 15.31, to 807.74.

2:08: Bankers Trust cuts its broker-loan rate to 11¾% from 12½%.

2:30: The Industrial Average is up 21.59 points, to 814.02.

3:29: Citibank cuts its prime to 14% from 14½%.

3:30: The Industrial Average is up 25.21, to 817.64.

4:27: The stock market officially chalks up a record rise on near-record volume. The rise in the Dow Jones Industrial Average is 38.81 points, with a close of 831.24. Volume is 92,860,000 shares.

Figure 1.5 The New York Times, August 18, 1982.

(The Wall Street Journal © 1982, Dow Jones & Company)

The bond market also enjoyed a massive rally. The *New York Times* reported that "bond prices soared and interest rates plunged as the credit markets turned in one of the sharpest single-day rallies on record. Dealers reported heavy trading volume in almost all sectors of the market," with most short-term rates falling by more than half a point. "The bond rally," the *Times* continued, "swept hundreds of millions of dollars of new corporate debt offerings to quick sellouts." These included $100 million offerings by Anadarko Production Co. and Avco Financial Services, Inc. Salomon itself greeted heavy demand for its $1 billion offering of "tigers"—zero-coupon certificates backed by US Treasuries, a brand-new kind of security rolled out by Merrill Lynch just the previous week.

The rally also proved to have "legs" by traveling in space and time. In London, new hopes for lower interest rates drove up the *Financial Times* industrial index in London by more than 2 percent (to 558.2) on August 18. (Stocks listed on Tokyo's Nikkei-Dow Jones index fell, however, because of a weakening yen.) In the United States, the S&P peaked for the month on August 23 at 118, or 14.5 percent higher than the closing price the night before my announcement.

When I returned to New Jersey that evening, several reactions to the day raced through my mind. I was most astonished by the magnitude of the apparent market reaction to my bullish announcement. I had not been the first to predict an overall reversal in the direction of interest rates. The afternoon's media reaction also surprised me, even though by then I was being quoted in the financial press almost daily. I mulled over the day's major political, business, and financial developments in search of other explanations for the markets' ending in record territory. Was it possible that my pronouncement was the precipitating cause? The next day would bring more answers.

August 17, 1982

Salomon Brothers Inc

One New York Plaza
New York, NY 10004
(212) 747-7000

Henry Kaufman

The Prospects for Interest Rates

Recent events in the economy and financial markets necessitate a fresh look at the prospects for U.S. interest rates. These events suggest that the present decline in interest rates will continue, although irregularly, with perhaps some dramatic interruptions. The decline in interest rates, and the length of time such a decline will take, will largely be determined by both the extent to which the U.S. credit structure has been impaired and the level of interest rates that will rejuvenate sustained economic activity. In this context, conventional cyclical benchmarks are no guide. On balance, some interest rate benchmarks for the next 12 months are as follows: long-term U.S. Government bonds now yielding 12¼% will fall into the 9%-10% range; the Federal funds rate now at 10% will decline to a low of 6%-7%.

A smart recovery in economic activity in the second half of this year is not likely to materialize. This removes the immediate threat to long-term interest rates. Consumer spending, although holding at a high plateau, has failed to respond to tax initiatives, while the rest of the economy is straitjacketed by financial blockages and fierce international competition. Generally, poor economic prospects also make businessmen less confident that the economy will be able to support substantially higher prices. Thus, inflation expectations will erode gradually. Significant economic expansion will require further declines in interest rates and considerable time to unwind the major financial impediments.

The refurbishing of business balance sheets and the rekindling of profitability are now overriding priorities of corporate management. These priorities cannot be quickly set aside. The corporate financial structure has become extremely fragile: corporate debt is top-heavy, resulting in widespread credit quality deterioration; and corporate profits have been waning since 1979. This shift in priorities has resulted in efforts to reduce inventories and, more recently, to cut back capital outlays. These measures will contribute not only to a stagnant economy, but also to a sharp contraction in business external financing. In the past, reduced business borrowing has been an important contributing factor to the fall in long-term interest rates.

Major financial institutions are not in any position to implement aggressive lending and investing strategies. A fall in interest rates will encourage thrift institutions to improve their liquidity and to minimize the risks in their long-term assets. Therefore, no new boom in housing activity is likely. Also, commercial banks are hamstrung by a thin capital base as well as by substantial non-earning assets, which may actually increase if the economy does not rebound rapidly. Even insurance companies are forced to cope with unprecedented cash flow and profitability problems.

The massive international debt overhang restricts the stimulative capacity of both domestic and international financial institutions. Stagnation here and abroad is self-reinforcing. The strength of the dollar, despite falling U.S. interest rates, will probably mean that American goods and services will become less competitive in international markets, and this, in turn, will cause more credit problems.

Interruptions in the decline in interest rates in the months ahead will
depend upon a number of critical considerations. First, there is the extent
to which monetary policy reverts to the enforcement of monetarism. It will
be difficult for the Fed to discern whether spurts in the money supply are
due to technical factors or to new underlying demands from a growing
economy. A prompt response by the Fed will temporarily push the funds
rate up, stalling the funding of liabilities and the general reliquefication
needed to bring the economy out of the doldrums. A significant lift in short
rates will interrupt the rally in long bonds, causing a narrowing in the
sharply sloped positive yield curve. However, this interruption is likely to
be temporary because the reliquefication needs of the economy will also be
stymied.

Second, the huge budget deficit is another factor that will periodically
interrupt the bond rally. Signs of business recovery and large new U.S.
Treasury issues will induce investor cautiousness because they will bring
about fears of crowding out. Large Treasury deficits will also limit the
ability of the Fed to follow a consistently easier policy. For the foreseeable
future, there will be a massive supply of high-quality U.S. Government
securities.

* * * * *

Salomon Brothers Inc
One New York Plaza
New York, NY 10004

Salomon Brothers Inc

Atlanta	Boston
Chicago	Dallas
Hong Kong	London (affiliate)
Los Angeles	San Francisco
Tokyo (representative office of affiliate)	

First Class Mail
US Postage
Paid
New York, NY
Permit No 8155

Figure 1.6 Salomon Brothers clients received this more formal version
of my memo. (*Courtesy Collection of Henry Kaufman*)

Chapter 2

The Press Reaction

The near chaos I encountered after returning to my office Tuesday morning only intensified on Wednesday, August 18. As I tried to resume my regular duties, colleagues continued to pop into my office with words of congratulations, and I held impromptu huddles with various combinations of the firm's senior partners. There was in fact little to do but respond to the flood of new business, and we all agreed to allow our public relations firm, Adams & Rinehart, to field interview requests.

We continued to decline all such requests for at least the first week, for several practical reasons. For one thing, the announcements to external clients and customers and to internal salespeople and dealers were clear enough on my revised position; elaboration would have been gilding the lily. For another, we saw no practical way to handle the deluge. Given the number of requests that flooded in, I easily could have spent weeks doing interviews, even if we limited the scope to the top-tier news outlets. And we risked offending some by selecting others. So our strategy was that I would do my best to get back to work, and hold off from my usual practice of regularly giving interviews or quotations until the fervor over this particular episode subsided.

We had to wait longer than expected. A full week following the big day, interview requests were still pouring in. Thanks to an unusual document that has survived the intervening four decades, we have a detailed picture of that week's bustle. On August 24, 1982, Mel Adams sent me a roster of his liaison with the press during the previous week. He had recorded every request, including the name of each newspaper, magazine, radio station, or television program, plus the name of the individual who called from each and—because many reporters and journals called multiple times—the number of contacts from each.

Not surprisingly, press writers made up the largest group. From the nation's financial capital, Jim Grant from *Barron's*; Tim Carrington, Dan Hertzberg, and Ed Foldessy of the *Wall Street Journal*; and a persistent John Henry of the *Daily News* phoned in. Not surprisingly, the city's (some would say the nation's) flagship newspaper, the *New York Times*, racked up the most calls, from Mike Quint (who regularly covered me), Tom Leak, Bob Bennett, and Doug Martin. Reporters from the leading wire services—the Associated Press, Dow Jones, UPI, Munifacts News Wire, and Reuters—also reached out to us. Calls poured in from major business and finance magazines such as *Business Today* (Tom Perlmutter), *Commodities Magazine*, *Commodity News*, *Fortune* (Mary Greenbaum), and *National Thrift News* (David Stahl). From the nation's leading general circulation magazines, Tom Tarnowsky phoned from *Time* and Eric Ipsen from *Newsweek*.

Adams & Rinehart, Inc.
708 Third Avenue
New York, New York 10017
212 557 0100

August 24, 1982

MEMORANDUM

TO: Henry Kaufman

FROM: Mel Adams

Following is a list of the media people who called us in response to your memo on interest rates. Calls for interviews continued over the weekend and through today. As you are aware, _all_ requests for interviews and statements were declined.

Please note that the first calls resulted from rumors on the Street very soon after the manifold on your preliminary draft text was issued. As on past occasions, customers and/or dealers were quick to advise certain press people before the Firm's own sales people were able to complete most of their calls. The number in brackets after the name indicates the number of calls to our office made by each.

THE PRESS

Associated Press
Steve Rosenfield   (3)
Lorraine Chichowski   (1)

Atlanta Journal
Emily Rubin   (1)

Barron's
Jim Grant   (2)

Bergen Record
Mr. Stepnowski   (2)

Boston Globe
Bob Lenzner   (1)

Bureau of National Affairs
Debbie Marchini   (1)

Business Today
Tom Perlmutter   (1)

Canadian Business Magazine
Harlowe Unger   (1)

Canadian News Service
Mike Isegrau   (1)

Figure 2.1 Mel Adams, who handled public relations for Salomon Brothers, recorded in extraordinary detail the interview requests that flooded our office. (*Courtesy Collection of Henry Kaufman*)

Chicago Tribune
Al Nagelberg   (1)
Terry Atlas   (1)
Laurie Cohen   (4)

Commodities Magazine
Mark Davis   (1)

Commodity News
Wyla Eason   (1)

Daily News
John Henry   (3)

Daily Telegraph (London)
Bill Langley   (1)

Dallas Times Herald
Janet Novak   (1)

Dow-Jones
Matt Winkler   (2)
Randy Forsyth   (2)

The Economist (London)
Bob Lenzner   (1)

The Financial Post (Toronto)
Barry Critchley   (2)

Financial Times of Canada
Deborah McGregor   (1)

The Financial Times (London)
Richard Lambert   (3)
Peter Clark   (1)
David Palmer   (1)

Fortune
Mary Greenbaum   (1)

Hartford Courant
Chris Oppenheimer   (1)

International Monetary Fund   (1)
Charles Gardner

Istoe (Brazil)
Eugenia Fernandez   (1)

Japan Economic Journal
Pat Glennon   (1)

Jiji Press
Ken Hanyu   (3)

Journal do Brazil
Frederico Utzieri   (1)

Kyoto News Service
Tadao Izuka   (2)

L'Economique (Paris)
Vincent Jouvert   (1)

London Daily Mail
Richard Leigh   (1)

Los Angeles Herald Examiner
Mike Schroder   (1)

Los Angeles Times
Bob Magnusson   (2)

The Manchester Guardian (U.K.)
Alex Brummer   (1)

The Melbourne Herald (Australia)
Barry Muir   (3)
Peter Custer   (1)

Munifacts News Wire
Stan Rosenberg   (2)

Nashville Banner
Sean Corrigan   (1)

National Thrift News
David Stahl   (1)

Newsweek
Tom Tarnowsky   (2)
Eric Ipsen   (2)

New York Magazine
Jack Egan   (1)

New York Post
Charles Koshetz   (1)
Alice Kipperman   (2)

The New York Times
Mike Quint   (1)
Tom Leak   (1)
Bob Bennett   (3)
Doug Martin   (1)

The Observer (London)
Carol Korzeniowsky   (1)

Philadelphia Inquirer
Craig Stock   (1)
Brian Sullivan   (2)

Reuters
Alex Nickoll   (2)
John Wallace   (1)

Sigma Photo News
J. P. Pappis   (1)

Time Magazine
Fred Ungerheuer   (1)
Owen Franken   (1)

Toronto News
Frank Tobi   (1)

Toronto Star
Jim Daw   (1)

United Press International
Mary Tobin   (3)

The Vancouver Sun
Der Hoi-Yin   (1)

Wall Street Journal
Tim Carrington   (1)
Dan Hertzberg   (2)
Ed Foldessy   (2)

Wall Street Journal (Chicago)
Tom Petzinger   (1)

The Washington Post
Meg Greenfield   (1) (requested an
                                                   Op-Ed page article)

Merrill Brown   (1)
Caroline Atkinson   (1)

Washington Times
Ken Hanner   (2)
Steve Beckner   (1)

BROADCASTING

ABC Network News
Phil Greer   (1)
Karen Ryan   (1)

ABC Radio News
Michael Jackson   (1)
Bill Flohr   (1)

ABC-TV Network News
Dan Cordtz   (4)
Ted Koppel   (1)
Mike Connor   (2)

ABC-TV "Nightline"
Nadine Muchin   (3)

Australian Broadcasting
Ian MacIntosh   (1)
Sue Cameron   (1)

Barry Gray Show
David Voycheimer   (1)

BBC
Eamon Fingleton   (2)
Elizabeth Cretch   (1)
Frances Halewood   (1)
Carol Fisk   (1)
Virginia Bailey (Washington)   (1)
David Taylor (Washington)   (2)

BBC "Financial World Tonight" (U.K.)
Ruth Corb   (1)
Peter Clark   (1)

Cable Network News
Mike Kandel   (1)
Tim Corbin   (1)
Nancy Lane   (1)
Kathy Pitorna   (1)

Canadian Broadcasting Company
Mr. Hurku   (2)
Donato Rogacki   (1)

CBS-TV
Dave Marash   (1)
Michael Glantz   (1)

CBS-TV Morning News
Steve Warner   (1)

CBS-TV Network News
Ray Brady   (2)
Grace Diekaus   (1)
Cynthia Ebbing   (1)

CBS Radio News
Michael Lynn   (1)
Mark Kiefting   (1)
Rob Forman   (1)

CBS Radio - KMOX (St. Louis)
Peggy Cohill   (1)

Channel 5-TV
Celeste Whiteford   (1)
Dick McIntire   (1)
Bert Kearns   (1)

Channel 11-TV
Felix Martinez   (1)

Chicago TV News
Terry Russelb   (1)

C-Span Cable News
Gail Rubin   (1)

The David Brinkley ABC-TV Sunday Program
Veronique Rodman   (2)

Dow-Jones Radio
Sam Alcorn   (2)
Larry Kofsky   (1)

Financial News Network
Wes Archie   (1)
Liebe Geste   (1)

"Good Morning America" (ABC-TV)
Mike Kelly   (1)

Independent Network News
Bill Dudar   (2)

London Radio Broadcasting
David Loyn   (1)
Jane Davis   (1)

MacNeil-Lehrer (Channel 13)   (1)

Mutual Radio Network (Washington)
Greg Hernandez   (1)

NBC Network News
Tom Kelly   (2)
Len Tepper   (1)
Davis Hazinsky   (1)
Tom Sullivan (California)   (1)

NBC Radio (Washington)
Sol Levine   (1)

NBC-TV News
Bob Temple   (1)

Radio News Network
Arlo Sederberg   (1)

The Voice of America
Al Pessin   (1)

WABC Radio
Gus Engelman   (1)

Wall Street Journal Radio Network
Larry Kofsky   (2)

Wall Street Week
Rich Dubroff   (1)

WGST Radio (Georgia)
Dennis O'Hare   (1)

WMCA
Neil Fleeger   (1)

WPIX
Brook Allen   (1)

cc: J. H. Gutfreund

From outside New York, we heard from leading newspapers based in other major US cities: Atlanta (the *Journal*), Boston (the *Globe*), Chicago (three reporters from the *Tribune*, with the very persistent Laurie Cohen putting in four requests, along with a request from the Chicago office of the *Wall Street Journal*), Dallas (the *Times Herald*), Los Angeles (the *Herald Examiner* as well as Bob Magnusson of the *L.A. Times*), and Philadelphia (Brian Sullivan and Craig Stock at the *Inquirer*).

In the nation's capital, Ken Hanner and Steve Beckner (a long-time Fed watcher) reached out from the *Washington Times*, while three reporters from the *Post* phoned in, including Mary Ellen "Meg" Greenfield, who four years earlier had won a Pulitzer Prize for Editorial Writing. Charles Gardner from the International Monetary Fund asked to speak with me. Several smaller city newspapers bravely jostled for interviews as well, from the nearby *Record* of Hackensack, New Jersey, to dailies from Hartford and Nashville. Even the modest *Sigma Photo News*, catering to photographers, gave it a shot.

I was especially gratified—and more than a little surprised—to learn of the scope of international coverage. London, as the world's second greatest financial center, was home to many business and financial writers eager to debrief me about the August 17 financial tsunami. Richard Lambert, recently appointed financial editor of the *Financial Times*, phoned in three times. He would later serve as the paper's editor (1991–2001) and was knighted in 2011. Two of his colleagues from the *Times* also phoned, as did Carol Korzeniowsky from *The Observer*; Richard Leigh from the *London Daily Mail*; Bill Langley from the *Daily Telegraph*; and Bob Lenzner, a prominent business journalist then at the *Economist*. To the north, the *Manchester Guardian* reached out. Canada was well represented among the solicitors, with half a dozen news outlets phoning in. Calls also came as far away as Australia, Japan (three), Brazil (two), and France. Although no German news outlets were listed in the Adams memo, German business writers (who, I suspected, gave me special coverage for a long time because of my name and origins) quickly got to work writing stories about the August 17 boom, as some of the headlines in this chapter show.

By August 24, Adams & Rinehart had collected interview requests (some of them repeats) from seventy-four print journalists working at fifty-three news outlets.

Then there were the requests for on-air interviews from broadcast networks at home and abroad: a total of sixty-five television and radio journalists working for thirty-eight different networks. I had been appearing fairly regularly on some of the more business- and finance-oriented networks and programs (such as PBS's *Wall Street Week with Louis Rukeyser*), but the impact of August 17 attracted the attention of bigger fish. These included ABC's *Nightline*, the BBC's *Financial World Tonight*, the *CBS Morning News*, and ABC's *Good Morning America* and its Sunday program with David Brinkley.

Unable to interview me, print journalists forged ahead without fresh quotations. The result was hundreds of domestic and foreign stories. Our firm's clipping service typically filled one thick bound volume of clippings about my newspaper and magazine coverage for each year. Stories from the second half of August 1982 *alone* now filled an entire volume.

The August 17 market boom tended to amplify the sorts of coverage I had been getting already. Of course, it was easy enough for writers to play off the Dr. Doom/Dr. Gloom theme by using the "hook" of their stories that—finally, finally—I was no longer gloomy about interest rates! The long-standing guru/wizard theme was infused with new life. Nearly all the press accounts ascribed the August 17 bull market to the release of my memo, although a few accounts also noted its combined effect with Al Wojnilower's memo from the previous day (see the end of chapter five) or President Reagan's comments on deficit reduction.

Here is a representative sample of headlines and other items from US and foreign publications, most of them written about the August 17 bull market.

Trading Is Heavy
Bond Prices Soar and Rates Plunge In One of Biggest Rallies on Record

Figure 2.2 When a financial record is broken, *The Wall Street Journal* never misses it. (August 18, 1982) *(The Wall Street Journal © 1982, Dow Jones & Company)*

Figure 2.3 *The New York Times, August 18, 1982. (From The New York Times. © 1982 The New York Times Company. All rights reserved. Used under license. www.nytimes.com)*

INTEREST PLUNGES, ELEVATING STOCKS TO A RECORD GAIN

REVISED FORECAST NOTED

Drop in High Rates Attributed to Stubborn Recession and Reduced Loan Demand

MAN IN THE NEWS

Megastar of Wall Street

BY RICHARD LAMBERT

Wall St surge as Kaufman predicts interest rate fall

Financial Times Thursday August 19 1982

NEW YORK MARKETS

Wild times on Wall Street

By Richard Lambert in New York

Figure 2.6 *Financial Times, August 19, 1982. (Used under licence from the Financial Times. All Rights Reserved.)*

Wall St. gains record 38.81

Figure 2.7 *Financial Times, August 19, 1982. (Used under licence from the Financial Times. All Rights Reserved.)*

Figure 2.8 *The New York Times, August 18, 1982. (From The New York Times. © 1982 The New York Times Company. All rights reserved. Used under license. www.nytimes.com)*

Some economists say that Kaufman's change of mind on interest rates came late and that his influence may wane.

Henry Kaufman:
Spark for a Rally

Industrials Rise Record 38.81 Points
In Second-Heaviest Big Board Day

Figure 2.9 The Wall Street Journal, August 18, 1982. (The Wall Street Journal © 1982, Dow Jones & Company)

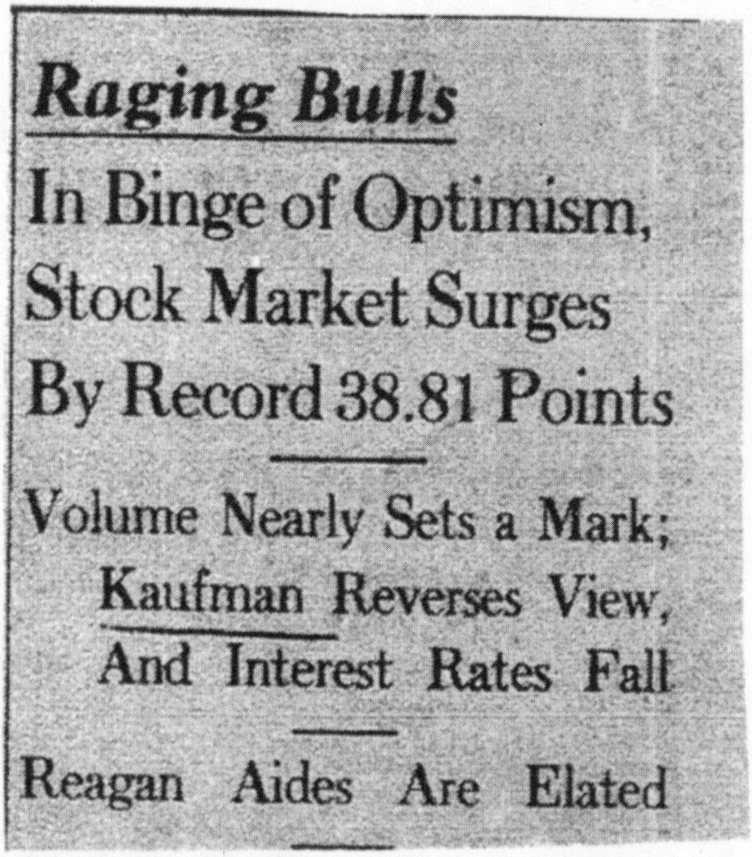

Raging Bulls
In Binge of Optimism,
Stock Market Surges
By Record 38.81 Points

Volume Nearly Sets a Mark;
Kaufman Reverses View,
And Interest Rates Fall

Reagan Aides Are Elated

Figure 2.10 The Wall Street Journal, August 18, 1982. (The Wall Street Journal © 1982, Dow Jones & Company)

Dow Soars by 38.81; Volume Near Peak

Increase Best Ever as Prices Rise on Falling Interest Rates

Figure 2.11 *The New York Times, August 18, 1982. (From The New York Times. © 1982 The New York Times Company. All rights reserved. Used under license. www.nytimes.com)*

Stock Market Records Its Largest Jump Ever

Figure 2.12 *The New York Times, August 18, 1982. (From The New York Times. © 1982 The New York Times Company. All rights reserved. Used under license. www.nytimes.com)*

The Washington Post

AN INDEPENDENT NEWSPAPER

Euphoria on Wall Street

Figure 2.13 *The Washington Post, August 18, 1982. (From The Washington Post. © 1982. All rightsreserved. Used under license. www.washingtonpost.com)*

Courier ★ EXPRESS

ESTABLISHED 1834   ESTABLISHED 1846

A-10   TUESDAY, AUGUST 24, 1982

When Henry Speaks. . .

EDITORIAL

Untutored laymen (or "lambs") must regard with awe the power of Henry Kaufman, who looks like the corner druggist and sends the stock market soaring or plummeting at his whim. Some Dow by 31 and 30 points in 1979 and 1981. "It's unfortunate," sniffed one rival broker, "that investors rely so heavily on one individual and seem unable to perceive for themselves funda-

Figure 2.14 Buffalo Courier Express, August 24, 1982. (Courtesy of the Archives & Special Colellctions Department, E.H. Butler Library , SUNY Buffalo State)

THE WALL STREET JOURNAL, THURSDAY, AUGUST 19, 1982

REVIEW & OUTLOOK

Dr. Doom's Rally

Figure 2.15 The Wall Street Journal, August 19, 1982. (The Wall Street Journal © 1982, Dow Jones & Company)

Figure 2.16 With a captivating collage and a well-turned title, this op-ed nicely captured the story. *The Philadelphia Inquirer*, August 19, 1982. *(From* The Philadelphia Inquirer. © 1982. All rights reserved. Used under license. www.inquirer.com*)*

KAUFMAN STILL SEES 9-10 PC
LONG RATES - 7 PC FED FUNDS
-3 11 EST-
- -
KAUFMAN PREDICTS DISCOUNT RATE
CUT TODAY OR MONDAY
-3 12 EST-

KAUFMAN - INTEREST RATES

DALLAS -DJ- SALOMON BROTHERS ECONOMIST HENRY KAUFMAN TOLD A REGIONAL INVESTMENT CONFERENCE HERE THAT 'I STILL THINK INTEREST RATES WILL GO DOWN IN THE NEAR TERM.'
HE REITERATED HIS MID-AUGUST FORECAST THAT FEDERAL FUNDS WOULD FALL TO 'AT LEAST 7 PC' FROM A CURRENT 9 1-8 PC AND LONG-TERM GOVERNMENT BOND RATES WOULD FALL TO 9-10 PC FROM THE CURRENT 10.60 PC.
THAT FORECAST WAS BASED MOSTLY ON KAUFMAN'S ANALYSIS THAT THE ECONOMY IS EXTREMELY WEAK AND THAT CREDIT DEMAND PARTICULARLY FROM BUSINESS CORPORATIONS WILL NOT PICK UP VERY FAST.
HE SAID HOWEVER FACTORS THAT MIGHT DRIVE INTEREST RATES UP ARE A RISE IN THE COST OF HOUSING FINANCE AND THE AMOUNT OF EXTERNAL FINANCING BY BUSINESS CORPORATIONS WHICH HE DESCRIBED AS 'ONE OF THE CRITICAL FACTORS' IN A POSSIBLE REBOUND IN RATES.
KAUFMAN SPOKE TO ABOUT 300 ECONOMISTS AND BUSINESS LEADERS AT A SALOMON BROTHERS SOUTHWEST INVESTMENT CONFERENCE.
- 3 27 PM EST NOV 5-82

KAUFMAN - DISCOUNT RATE

DALLAS -DJ- SALOMON BROTHERS ECONOMIST HENRY KAUFMAN AT A REGIONAL INVESTMENT CONFERENCE PREDICTED THE FEDERAL RESERVE WOULD CUT THE DISCOUNT RATE TODAY OR MONDAY TO 9 PC OR AS LOW AS 8 1-2 PC FROM THE CURRENT 9 1-2 PC.
KAUFMAN SAID THE FED CAN'T AFFORD TO DISAPPOINT EXPECTATIONS IN THE MARKETS OF A CONTINUING DECLINE IN SHORT-TERM RATES. THESE EXPECTATIONS 'WILL VIRTUALLY INDUCE TH CENTRAL BANK TO CUT THE DISCOUNT RATE' HE SAID.
HE SAID THE RALLIES IN THE BOND AND STOCK MARKETS ARE DEPENDENT TO A LARGE EXTEN ON THE BELIEF THAT THE DECLINE IN SHORT-TERM RATES ISN'T OVER.
-0- 3 20 PM EST NOV 5-82

Figures 2.17 and 2.18 News of the record day went international quickly, thanks to the wire service telegraphs and teletypes deployed years before the Internet. (Courtesy Collection of Henry Kaufman)

Forecast Launched Rally

Seer Talks, Dow Listens

Figure 2.19 Almost as often as I was called "Dr. Doom," I was labeled a wizard, guru, soothsayer, or seer. It wasn't magic; it was mathematics. *The Los Angeles Times,* August 18, 1982. *(The Associated Press)*

HENRY WHO?

KAUFMAN...the man who started the recovery in the world's sharemarkets. A man with more financial credibility than any world leader

Figure 2.20 My name was foreign to many Europeans, yet sometimes the Dr. Doom label traveled overseas. *The Sydney Morning Herald,* August 1982. *(Courtesy the Sydney Morning Herald)*

Part II

Why It Happened

Chapter 3

Intellectual Roots

As the research departments at Salomon Brothers grew in size and international reputation, I emerged as the firm's leading public voice on economics and finance. Along with my own analysis, I drew on the work of scores, eventually hundreds, of researchers and specialists, many of whom went on to build exceptional careers. Internally, I represented their interests—especially their independence—in the highest echelons of the firm as a member of its Executive Committee.

Externally, I became the figurehead for all the work we did. But in the end, I alone was responsible for what went into the memoranda and reports I signed, what I told major clients, and the public pronouncements I made to the media. Whenever I changed my views on financial markets in any significant way, I memorialized it in writing. It is hardly surprising—human nature, really—that the media and financial audiences would want to personalize or humanize what appeared in my memos and reports.

Here, I recount some of the major influences that shaped my views on economics and finance. Some might consider these biases; I prefer to regard them as shaping experiences and orientations. All of us need ways of making sense of the world, and those begin to form at an early age. These early influences contributed to my later unorthodox stance, which helps explain why the reaction to my August 17, 1982, memo was so enormous.

In one of my earlier books, *On Money and Markets: A Wall Street Memoir* (2000), I wrote about the profound influences of my early childhood in the German village of Wenings. I lived in a loving, extended family supported by a cattle trading and butchering business. But my grandfather, after laboring for decades to accumulate assets worth some 200,000 marks, was forced to start over when the economy of the Weimar Republic (1919–1933) began its harrowing demise in the 1920s. Night after night my grandfather told vivid stories—of customers unable to pay their accounts or paying them off with virtually worthless currency because of hyperinflation, and of rising social unrest and anti-Semitism. After a night of village terror in 1937, when Nazis ransacked our house, we fled for our lives. I was nine years old, but old enough to understand that collapsing currency and banks could destroy a society.

After we settled in America, initially in the East Bronx, we relocated to the Washington Heights section of upper Manhattan, an enclave for many middle-class German Jewish families. I studied hard at the then well-regarded George Washington High School (where Henry Kissinger and Alan Greenspan had preceded me by four years and one year, respectively) and considered a career in medicine. But soon after starting my college career at the University Heights campus of New York University in the Bronx, I became enthralled with economics as well as

Figure 3.1 After World War II, George Washington High School was a training ground for many later-successful figures. *(Wurts Bros. [NY, NY]. Museum of the City of New York)*

banking and finance. After graduating with a BA in economics in 1948, I enrolled in a Master's of Science program—this time in finance—at Columbia University, and completed the degree the following year. Following a brief search, I landed a position as a credit analyst for People's Industrial Bank (acquired by Manufacturers Hanover in 1953), where I remained until early 1957. But my desire for deeper knowledge of finance inspired me to enroll in the PhD program in banking and finance at NYU's Graduate School of Business Administration. While continuing to work, I attended night classes for half a dozen years at 90 Trinity Place in Manhattan's Financial District.

There I became a student of NYU's by-then legendary professor of finance, Marcus Nadler. Although Professor Nadler commanded deep and broad knowledge across the spectrum of finance and economics, two aspects of his approach especially shaped my progress as a budding economist: his belief in the value of history for understanding contemporary issues in banking and finance; and his recognition that a sound and stable financial system was key to a society's health, well-being, and economic democracy. The latter insight resonated deeply with what I had heard my grandfather speak about so often back in Germany. Now, in the classrooms of NYU—then one of the top American universities in business and finance (among other subjects)—I was learning more formally about the economic processes that brought my homeland to its knees and tore apart its social fabric.

Marcus Nadler was born and raised in a rural mountainous region of the Austro-Hungarian Empire. Academically precocious, he earned one of the few positions at the University of Vienna that Emperor Franz Joseph reserved for Eastern European Jews. But his college career was interrupted by the Great War. While serving as an officer, he was captured and shipped to a prison camp in Siberia. To help tolerate the boredom and deprivations of incarceration, he passed the hours studying English. Following the Russian Revolution, the new Soviet Socialist Republic quit the war under the terms of the March 1918 Treaty of Brest-Litovsk. Like growing numbers of Jews, Nadler feared for his future in Europe. Waiting in Manchuria until the war ended, he headed for the United States.

Once on American shores, Nadler began working in the New York City Post Office and before long began attending Columbia University. Nadler then landed a banking job, and after a few years at that position, moved to Washington, DC, to work for the Fed. Sometime after 1926 he transferred to NYU. As recounted by his son, Paul (who later also taught banking and finance), "My father's big break came when New York University was starting an institute to determine the worth of defaulted foreign bonds. Every country owed money to the United States after World War

Figure 3.2 Marcus Nadler in his office overlooking the Trinity Church Cemetery and Mausoleum, New York University Graduate School of Business Administration, 1946. "If ever I start feeling too important," Nadler reflected from that perch, "all I have to do is look out the window." (*Marcus Nadler and the Money Marketeers, A Unique Story in American Education*/Salomon Bros., NY)

I, but no one was paying except Finland. To run the institute, NYU needed someone who knew Europe, knew finance, and could develop statistics and studies for bond holders."

The dean of NYU's School of Commerce, Accounts, and Finance who hired him, John T. Madden, overlooked Nadler's still-rough command of English and recognized his potential beyond research as a classroom teacher. And indeed, Nadler soon established himself as one of the most erudite and captivating lecturers on campus, with classrooms packed not only with matriculating students but also many auditors and spectators who came just to listen and learn. It was an eventful period in economic history, with the fates of nations still rising and falling. Nadler's clear and powerful lectures helped make sense of it all for large audiences of New Yorkers, including me, and it was said he never delivered the same lecture twice.

A few years after he was hired by NYU, Nadler was invited to co-author new editions of *Money and Banking,* a six-hundred-page magnum opus and one of the most authoritative works on the subject in the English language. For Nadler and the other NYU financial experts, Germany offered the most sobering case of all from the vantage point of the early postwar period—and arguably still does to this day. For me, classroom learning at NYU was far from clinical and abstract.

Marcus Nadler's lectures on Germany's interwar financial and economic travails naturally captivated me, but they were only one dimension of his many influences on my thinking. He spoke often about the extraordinary challenges involved in coordinating fiscal and monetary policy in the United States—a topic I would go on to speak and write about from the time I became the first "Fed watcher" at Salomon Brothers to my most recent book.

I also built on the work of Nadler and his NYU colleagues regarding the limitations of the concept of asset marketability. Pointing to the effects of panics and depressions, they had written in 1947, "Experience during major panics and depressions, particularly that of 1930–1933, has given repeated blows to the 'shiftability' theory of commercial banking, and has tended at least to *refute the contention that marketability is the equivalent of true liquidity in banking assets* [emphasis added]. Such experience has shown that long-term securities are subject to the risk of severe price declines, and that marketability may be impaired when there is a general rush to liquidate and little buying power available." As I later watched credit quality generally worsen in the late twentieth and early twenty-first centuries, I came to conclude that "the reality of a financial asset's marketability has shifted and no longer is well understood . . . [B]ecause private sector credit quality has deteriorated over the last few decades, there is now underlying uncertainty about how much can be traded *at a specific price over various phases of an interest rate cycle*." The causal drivers in Nadler's time were different, but the core concept is the same.

Although NYU professors and students shaped much of my early postwar thinking about economics and finance, there were other less direct but important influences as well. Several public intellectuals—scholars who wrote accessible, widely discussed books—come to mind. One was yet another Austrian economist (who, like Nadler, graduated from the University of Vienna and eventually settled in the United States), Friedrich August von

Hayek. In 1944, Hayek published, first in Britain and then in the US, a book that would spark international debate about the relationship between political and economic freedom. I had read *The Road to Serfdom* during my early days at NYU, and today the book is considered a key text in the classical liberal tradition dating back to Adam Smith and John Locke. But that shorthand categorization oversimplifies both the book's message and its appeal to me and to millions of other post–World War II readers who did not identify with either end of the political spectrum.

Along with Hannah Arendt, Ayn Rand, and several other European intellectuals (many of them Jewish) who emigrated to the United States during or after the Second World War, Hayek was gravely concerned about "collectivism"—political econo-mies that required individuals to subordinate their interests to the group and its charismatic leaders. These thinkers had seen up close the disastrous results as political and economic power were consolidated in Italy, Russia, and Germany. "The various kinds of collectivism, communism, fascism, etc., differ among them-selves in [their goals]," Hayek wrote. "But they all differ from liberalism and individualism in wanting to organize the whole of society and all its resources for this unitary end and in refusing to recognize autonomous spheres in which the ends of the individ-uals are supreme."

For Hayek, economic freedom was necessary for political freedom. This proposition, which continues to attract scholarly attention,* reinforced my thinking about the connection between

---

* In an important 2019 book, *Democracy and Prosperity: Reinventing Capitalism Through a Turbulent Century*, political economists Torben Iversen from Harvard and David Soskice from the London School of Economics argue that "very broadly, democracy and advanced

financial health and political and social stability. Like Hayek, I had first-hand experience with one of the most virulent forms of "collectivism" (National Socialism) and believed in the great virtues of capitalism: its ability to innovate and create wealth and its fundamental compatibility with democracy. But I also understood that highly unregulated markets (such as Wall Street in the 1920s) and currencies (as in late Weimar Germany) could lead to disaster.

I completed my PhD in banking and finance in 1958, a year after I landed a job (with Professor Nadler's help) at the Federal Reserve Bank of New York. Nearly five years later, again with Nadler's assistance, I joined Salomon Brothers, where I would remain for the next twenty-six years. Even though my formal education was complete, my intellectual growth continued—in part thanks to events sponsored by my new employer.

In the 1960s, economists were engaged in lively debate about the relative virtues of fiscalism versus monetarism. Some, working in the tradition of John Maynard Keynes, saw fiscal policy as the most important component of macroeconomic management, while the monetarists believed that interest rates and the money supply were king. For many years, Keynesianism had dominated, but by the mid-1960s monetarists—most notably Professor Milton Friedman at the University of Chicago—were rising in prominence. The two positions jostled very publicly in late 1968, when Friedman debated Walter Heller, a professor of economics at the University of Minnesota and the former

capitalism have been symbiotic in the advanced nation-states. Democracies positively reinforce advanced capitalism and well-functioning advanced capitalism reinforces democratic support" (p. xii).

chairman of the Council of Economic Advisers under presidents Kennedy and Johnson.

The forum intersected with my professional life in several ways. It took place at 100 Trinity Place, near Wall Street, and it was sponsored by NYU's Graduate School of Business Administration thanks to funding from Salomon Brothers, in honor of its founder. As the "Seventh Annual Arthur K. Salomon Lecture," the event attracted by far the largest audience in the history of the series, not only those of us who filled the Trinity Place lecture hall, but the many who watched the event on television monitors in overflow classrooms or tuned in to television or radio broadcasts.

Neither top economist argued that the other was completely wrong; rather, the debate was about whether the opponent's stance had been "oversold." Still, there were real differences between the two positions that held important policy consequences. For instance, Heller argued that the Federal Reserve should continually readjust (or "fine-tune") the money supply, whereas Friedman advocated setting it on a fixed trajectory to expand a few percentage points a year.

It is impossible to know how many minds the debate may have changed (the *New York Times* declared the debate "an even match"), but it was invigorating to see macroeconomic policy attract so much national attention—and deservedly so, for the stakes were high. By that time, I had concluded that strict monetarism was too formulaic and rigid; yet I also had serious reservations about the strong fiscalist approach. I was concerned that too many Keynesians had become irresponsible about deficit spending as a short-term measure for reviving the economy, and I doubted that some fiscal responses to unfavorable economic conditions could achieve their aims in the real world. The real challenge in the fiscal–monetary debate, it seemed to me, was how to coordinate the two so they did not work at cross purposes. The debate confirmed my developing view that money matters but credit counts.

Friedman-Heller Debate Proves an E

The great shoot-out at the corral on Trinity Place ended in a draw yesterday afternoon.

In one of the most sparkling and significant economic debates in recent years, Walter W. Heller, the nation's leading spokesman for the Keynesian "new economics," met Milton Friedman, the articulate leader of the monetarist school of economics, whose analyses have shaken concepts that long have been treated as accepted dogma in elementary textbooks.

The occasion was the seventh annual Arthur K. Salomon lecture at the New York University Graduate School of Business Administration, at 100 Trinity Place, next door to the American Stock Exchange.

The subject was the rela-

Dr. Milton Friedman, left, and Dr. Walter W. Heller before the lecture-debate yesterday

The New York Times (by Robert Walker)
Among those on hand for the lecture was Arthur Levitt, right foreground, glasses, the state controller. The session was held at the New York University Graduate School of Business Administration, at 100 Trinity Place, downtown.

Figure 3.3 In the 1960s I was excited to attend the famed Friedman–Heller debate and similar events sponsored by Salomon Brothers. *(From The New York Times. © 1982 The New York Times Company. All rights reserved. Used under license.)*

These influences on my upbringing and education did not pre-ordain my financial and economic views or forecasts, but were an inescapable backdrop that surely sensitized me to certain risks more than many others. In the next chapter, I consider how I became a leading authority on interest rates and financial markets, and why I tended to be more bearish than the mainstream. Both are important for understanding what happened on August 17, 1982.

Chapter 4

Why I Was Bearish for So Long

From a seven-person team in 1962, the fixed-income research operation at Salomon Brothers grew over the next two decades to become widely regarded as the best in the world. As the bond markets grew, others tried to emulate us in research, but never caught up. The reverse was true in equities research, where several other leading investment houses already had well-established capabilities by the time we entered the field, a lead we were unable to overcome.

Along the way, I emerged as the firm's most visible presence. And because my views often differed from the generally bullish outlook of most analysts, some began to refer to me as "Dr. Doom." To be sure, as the previous chapter chronicled, my formative years sensitized me to the societal dangers of financial instability. But I never considered myself inherently gloomy or bearish.

The main reason I attracted a large following on Wall Street wasn't because my forecasts often were cautionary and sometimes downright bearish—after all, no one likes bad news! Rather, it was because of my commitment to rigorous, objective research, which, especially during the tumultuous 1970s, frequently caused me to see dark clouds on the horizon while helping me build a highly regarded record. (Later in this chapter I recount the troubling signals I was reading, especially regarding interest rates, in the 1970s and early 1980s.)

I began monitoring developments in the financial markets when I started working at the Federal Reserve Bank of New York in 1957. After I moved to Salomon Brothers in 1962, I started following central banking closely, which made me one of a small number, probably no more than half a dozen, of early "Fed watchers." (According to business writer Martin Mayer, Billy Salomon believed that I was the very first.) Today, such

Figure 4.1 When I joined Salomon Brothers in 1962, I was mentored by Sidney Homer, the world's leading authority on the history of interest rates. *(Courtesy Collection of Henry Kaufman)*

analysts comprise a small army. But it wasn't until I joined Salomon Brothers that my career as a market analyst and, eventually, financial forecaster began in earnest.

Elsewhere I have written about Sidney Homer, from his family of distinguished musicians, to his completion of *A History of Interest Rates*—which soon became a classic— shortly after I joined Salomon. Along with Marcus Nadler, Homer became another major influence in my life. A Harvard graduate, Homer had worked in finance since 1923, then as president of his own firm (Homer & Company, Inc.) from 1932 to 1943, and then (after a stint with the Foreign Economic Administration) as manager of the institutional department at Scudder, Stevens & Clark from 1945 to 1961. Scudder had no research department at the time. Salomon Brothers recruited Homer with the offer of a partnership and the opportunity to found a research department, one of the first on Wall Street. Back then, it was quite unusual for a Wall Street firm to offer a partnership to a sixty-year-old, but the other Salomon partners—especially Charles Simon and William Salomon—recognized Homer's great value in establishing a research operation.

As for myself, given my education and experience, Salomon Brothers took a real risk hiring me. In his lively history of post–World War II American economists, Alfred Malabre (former economics editor for the *Wall Street Journal* and head of his own consulting firm since 1978) records that in US corporations, "economists played virtually no role at all in [the] early postwar years," including at financial firms, "where one would imagine there existed even then a special need for forecasting and number crunching." A. Gary Shilling, holding a Stanford economics

PhD, was recruited by Merrill Lynch, Pierce, Fenner & Smith in 1967, but remained there only until 1971 because, according to Malabre, "he attempted to take his role as in-house economist seriously" without upper management support. When I joined Salomon, few of the firm's partners even held an undergraduate college degree. In 1962 I was the first or one of the first recipients of a PhD to work on Wall Street.

That first year, Malabre visited Sidney Homer and me at Salomon Brothers, and later recalled his impressions: "When I first encountered these two men . . . they worked in small, cluttered offices, seemingly forgotten outposts of the securities firm, which could only be reached in labyrinthian fashion after circumventing the obstacle course presented by Salomon's sprawling trading floor."

One of the first assignments Sidney gave me was to monitor Federal Reserve and US Treasury operations in order to project the central bank's daily activities in the marketplace as well as its near-term financing requirements. I began to report these findings in an internal document that went to our traders and salespeople. (The first one of these appeared March 23, 1962, and was only two paragraphs long.) When we realized that these readers were copying my bulletins and mailing them to clients, Sidney suggested that I publish a more formal report. But he admonished me to keep the format short and compact—four pages, and six-and-a-half by eight-and-a-half inches, to be exact. That way, he explained, it would match the size of two of the firm's other publications (the weekly *Bond Market Roundup* and the monthly *Bond Market Review*) while staying small enough for clients to fold in half and carry in a pocket.

Comments on Credit was born. On the front page, I typically evaluated and discussed monetary policy. In the remaining three pages, I discussed developments in the capital markets—for example, trends in bank loans and investments, who was buying US government securities, the deterioration of municipal bond ratings, or business term loans. Over time, *Comments on Credit* built a readership of more than 25,000, mostly institutional clients in the US and abroad. As business writer Martin Mayer noted, publication of each new issue was "astonishingly newsworthy" within Wall Street circles. (*Comments on Credit* ran until March 18, 1988.) Sidney's marketing instincts also proved correct; over the years I encountered quite a few clients who pulled the publication out of a jacket pocket and proceeded to ask me questions about my commentary.

Another publication we launched a few years later also helped build my reputation on Wall Street and was called (after name changes) *Prospects for Financial Markets*. Sidney Homer had asked me to attend a luncheon to which he had invited a few representatives from insurance companies, banks, and perhaps other financial institutions. He showed them a sheet of paper he had prepared that listed the key demanders of credit—households, corporations, the federal government, municipalities, and the like—along with estimates of their historical demands. Below those, he had listed the major providers of credit. The historical data came from a Federal Reserve publication generally known as "Flow of Funds" (today it is called "Financial Accounts of the United States").

Sidney then turned the conversation to the question of what these flows might look like for the coming year. From their key positions at major financial institutions, the men around the table came up with some figures, and we had a lively discussion about each financial sector. But we all knew those were rough estimates. Because Sidney saw the limitations in that approach, he asked me to undertake a more formal, detailed flow of funds analysis and devise methods for estimating current demands for credit, sources of credit from financial intermediaries, and estimates one year into the future, then present all that data in a credit market format.

It took quite a while and the help of my new assistant, Jim McKeon, to create the credit flow model. By 1981, the report was known as *Prospects for Financial Markets*, and that year's edition was thirty-six pages long with thirteen statistical tables that showed the credit demands for key sectors of the economy, along with the financial intermediaries and households that would finance those demands, and the implications of those credit flows for interest rates.

My work on the project gave me a unique vantage point into the structure of financial markets and institutions. It made me aware of dynamic and static institutions, including which demanders and suppliers of credit could withstand credit restraint and which ones could not. I had been aware of the flow of funds data while at the Fed. But before *Prospects for Financial Markets*, no one at the Fed or anywhere else had fully put it to use as an analytical tool for projecting market prospects for the year ahead.

Flow of funds analysis also helped me enormously in making interest rate forecasts. To make sound predictions using credit flow analysis, I found Gross Domestic Product (GDP) and other major macroeconomic indices to be extremely helpful. Even so, I knew that standard measures such as GDP have severe limitations, so I also drew on consensus economic forecasts such as the one in the *Blue Chip Report*. In many instances, my interest rate forecasts hinged on calculating the volume of funds available from intermediaries. If they were inadequate, households (that is, individual investors) would need to finance their demands directly as buyers of bonds. When funds to be provided by households were very large, interest rates would have to rise sufficiently enough to attract those investors directly. Conversely, very small direct participation by households would support stable or lower interest rates.

Prospects also attracted wide attention in the financial community. Over time, the publication's release grew to become a

Figure 4.2 In the 1970s and 1980s I was a frequent commentor on news programs such as *Meet the Press* (above) and *Wall Street Week* with Louis Rukeyser. *(Courtesy Collection of Henry Kaufman, photo by John M. DiJoseph/Reni News Photos Inc.)*

major media event. Salomon Brothers typically invited a thousand or so of its clients to our presentation of the next year's report at the Waldorf-Astoria. The financial news feeds were international, reaching around the globe all the way to Australia. Meanwhile, "three or four times a week," journalist Martin Mayer recounted, "[Kaufman] would lunch or dine with important Salomon customers, usually at one of the firm's airy and elegant dining rooms on the floor above the main trading floor high in One New York Plaza. He traveled often to the firm's out-of-town branches, where ballrooms would be rented for his 'private briefings.'"

After an extremely fruitful decade at Salomon Brothers, Sidney Homer retired in 1971. From that point forward, I served as the firm's most prominent public authority, contacted by media for economic and financial projections and, later in the decade, quoted in the press almost daily. That same year, I was appointed to the firm's Executive Committee, its chief governing body under the still-existing partnership structure. This was a unique and important appointment that was championed by Charlie Simon and supported by Bill Salomon. Sidney Homer had not served on the Executive Committee, nor did I know of any other research head on Wall Street who had risen to the highest level of his or her firm.

I knew the increased power would help me represent the interests of the firm's research units, especially when it came to protecting the independence of the research function. That led to an intriguing dynamic. On the one hand, Salomon was establishing a reputation for the world's best fixed-income research, partly because of its independence. On the other hand, as our analysis and forecasters became more and more valuable, pressure to exploit them internally, rather than sharing them with clients and the broader public, likewise grew.

It was around that time that Bill Salomon asked me to take over the management of all our research units. He was especially concerned with equities research. As I noted, several leading Wall Street firms already were deeply entrenched in equities research by the time Salomon entered the business. One very practical consequence was that in order to become competitive quickly, we had to recruit top talent from other firms rather than cultivate it internally. I soon discovered equities research staffing to be time consuming and often frustrating. "Rainmakers" at other firms typically made heavy demands, and those who came over to Salomon had to be acculturated into our ways, down to how we presented our findings in reports.

These tensions were heightened by the fact that the 1970s were shaping up to be a treacherous decade economically. In retrospect, we now know that the early 1970s were a watershed both for the US economy and much of the world. From the end of the Second World War to 1974, US productivity rose at an annual average of 2.5 percent, real weekly wages at 3 percent, and real family income—one of the best measures of American economic well-being—also at about 3 percent per year on average. For a variety of reasons, including the 1973 global "oil shock," all of that changed for the worse in 1974, when productivity (a key driver of economic growth) fell to an annual growth rate of 0.7 percent, and real weekly wages fell each year on average by nearly 1 percent from 1974 to 1991. The greatest economic expansion in world history had given way to a disappointing period of stasis. All of this was inextricably tied in with financial markets, including interest rates. And, like all historical actors, we at the time lacked a clear vision of how the larger picture would take shape.

But it was my unconventional stance on interest rates in 1974 that helped solidify my reputation. In a *Sunday New York Times* essay that January, I warned that it was not the oil shortage—on the minds of so many those days—that posed the greatest economic threat going forward, but rather "the inability of governments here and elsewhere to deal effectively with inflation." The problem was so grave, I warned, that it "casts serious doubt on the current consensus economic outlook for 1974." Late that summer I told a reporter at *Newsweek* that "the danger that the economy may get out of hand is greater than at any time in my career. We are not living in ordinary times." And by that time, a few other economists were sounding warnings as well.

Normally the business cycle and interest rates tend to peak very closely to each other. That year, the business cycle peaked in January, but I remained bearish on interest rates for ten more months. And indeed, during that period the yield on US government bonds rose from 7.10 percent to 8.70 percent, while the yield on three-month Treasury bills climbed from 7.43 percent to 9.22 percent. Inflation was running extremely high (at about 10 percent), but so were corporate borrowing and credit demands, and commercial banks were aggressively issuing certificates of deposit. And whereas most experts thought the energy crisis would ease interest rate pressure, I believed that initially it was having the opposite effect.

While attending the IMF–World Bank meetings in Washington, DC, that fall, I decided to change my position on bonds to bullish. Market reaction to the two-page memo I released October 8 was immediate and strong: that day the yield on long government bonds fell from 8.49 percent to 8.16 percent, and the Dow surged 3.9 percent. Looking back, we could see that long government bonds had peaked (at 8.6 percent) in August, and continued to fall (unevenly) well into the next year.

In several key respects, this episode foreshadowed the event that is the subject of this book. I remained bearish against the tide, attracting doubts and renewed criticism for being "Dr. Doom." Once I switched my position, the announcement abruptly caused a large market rally. And looking back, the timing of my announcement with the secular decline in interest rates proved to be much more accurate than most who had followed the business cycle more closely.

In a 1975 talk, I reflected on that unusual dynamic in this way: "The strong force of the inflationary momentum did not end with the termination of the economic boom in 1973. It extended into the recession and is disturbingly visible now at the start of a new recovery." It was because of my close monitoring of debt structure that I had been able to make the timely call, and I saw this as a blind spot within both the monetarist and Keynesian schools of thought: "On the financial side, one of the most glaring gaps of both schools has been the failure to recognize the emergence of a heavy debt structure and its impediment to economic recovery."

As we entered the second half of the decade, I again found myself holding to a bearish position when most others saw hopeful signs. It was easy to be deceived, it seemed to me, by superficial signs and even traditional indicators of positive economic performance. As I explained in a March 1979 speech, "Business is doing exceedingly well. Consumer spending is well above expectations, and such prominent financial institutions as commercial banks and insurance companies are prospering . . . In nearly all instances, real growth, including total GNP, consumer spending, and business and residential investments, was much greater in 1978, and particularly in the fourth quarter, than in the terminal year or the final quarter of the five preceding business expansions."

So what could be the problem? Why was I still bearish? As I went on to explain, three powerful yet underappreciated dynamics were at work: "The most glaring difference . . . is our attitude towards the present inflation." For the first eight years of the decade, Fed Chairman Arthur F. Burns had toiled unsuccessfully to bring down inflation because of (as I described in my previous book) his "lack of vision and forceful leadership" there. Now businessman G. William Miller, one year into his own chairmanship when I gave this talk, was also proving unequal to the task.* This long and dismal record had caused inflationary expectations to become deeply ingrained, I explained: "Our perception of the power and determination that the Government will bring to bear to break the back of inflation" had been seriously eroded. At times like that, the deep-seated apprehensions about the potentially devastating effects of inflation that had been ingrained in me at an early age rose to the surface.

Second, I warned about excessive debt creation. Incremental financial deregulation (such as the repeal of Regulation Q, which

---

* I discuss the Fed chairmanship of both men in Kaufman, *Tectonic Shifts*, pp. 20–22.

had set limits on what banks could pay on savings and time deposits) was combining with financial innovation—"a plethora of new, highly marketable obligations, ranging from floating rate CDs to pass-through mortgages"—to create a wave of easy credit. Volume was up, quality down.

And that in turn was making it difficult for the central bank to restrain the growth of debt, especially among borrowers of poorer quality. My concern about such structural changes on Wall Street made me more bearish about interest rates than most others.

Through the late 1970s, I reiterated my concerns about interest rates again and again in *Prospects for Financial Markets*. For 1977, I predicted that both short- and long-term rates would rise, especially the former, which "should climb back to their 1976 highs in the year ahead." With some variation on timing and detail, my forecast for 1978 was the same: "Both long- and short-term interest rates will continue their recent rise." My analysis of flow of funds and other variables again led me to conclude that "all point to further sharp gains in the level of interest rates for most of 1979."

With Paul Volcker at the helm of the Fed beginning August 6, 1979, I began to hope for a solution to the inflation conundrum, but knew it would take time for his decisive actions to yield results. (Volcker's approach of holding the money supply stable while letting interest rates fluctuate ushered in a brief but severe economic contraction and ultimately worked against inflation.) As I wrote in the 1980 edition of *Prospects*, "The persistence of inflation in the early period of economic contraction will aggravate rather than ease the shortage of liquidity. Only later on, when business priorities have shifted to the restoration of financial adequacy, will tension lessen in the credit markets. If so, new postwar highs would be established for almost all interest rates somewhere before midyear."

At the beginning of 1981—and the start of President Ronald Reagan's administration, with its promises of renewed economic vigor and balanced budgets—I remained bearish on interest rates. "Rates will remain historically high," I wrote in *Prospects*, "but will be subject to extreme volatility. Long-term rates are likely to show on balance an irregular upward bias. This reflects an economy which will generate large net new borrowings needs, which, in turn, will provoke periodic attempts by the Federal Reserve to cap fresh inflationary impulses. There are also sizeable pent-up corporate demands for long-term funds."

Thus, Dr. Doom.

The late esteemed Harvard historian of early America, Bernard Bailyn, wrote about what he called "latent" history. By this he meant "historical events or developments that the participants were not themselves aware of—like shifts in the birth rate." In contrast, "most history," Bailyn noted, "concerns manifest events, public and private—events that people are keenly aware of, think about, struggle with." How do we get at "latent" history? It "emerges uniquely from quantification," Bailyn explained. He was referring to the practice among some economic and social historians of compiling and analyzing massive quantities of data to see broad patterns in demographics, population movements, standards of living, and the like.

In the summer and fall of 1981, both latent and manifest history were impinging on my professional life in very important ways. On the latent side, October would mark the high point in the secular peak of the yield on long-term US government bonds. It was my job to unearth such important trends, but it would be more than several months before I did so. One pressing reason was that the overt or "manifest" realities of daily life at Salomon Brothers began to take an important new direction, one that seemed to become almost all-encompassing: after more than seven decades, the Salomon Brothers partnership might merge and go corporate. This pulled me away from my primary task of analyzing financial markets and interest rates.

The incorporation of Salomon Brothers largely grew out of a fundamental change in strategic vision that came when John Gutfreund followed Billy Salomon as the firm's managing partner in 1978. Billy had encouraged members of the firm to compete aggressively, but only in ways that did not risk the integrity of the firm. He especially valued relationships with long-standing clients. Gutfreund took a more transactional approach that favored profit maximization, including greater risk taking.

My relationship with John long had been one of coexistence more than a close working relationship. In subtle and occasionally not-so-subtle ways, John had made it clear that he questioned the value of the firm's research operations and somewhat resented my high public profile. A few times during our regular Monday morning meetings with traders and salespeople, when I discussed the previous week's developments in financial markets and talked about prospects for the coming weeks, John made some off-handed and somewhat sarcastic remarks about my analysis in front of the audience. After this happened a second or third time, I responded by spontaneously quoting a few lines from my favorite poet, Alexander Pope:

Be sure your self and your own reach to know,
How far your genius, taste, and learning go;
Launch not beyond your depth, but be discreet,
And mark that point where sense and dullness meet.

The assembled audience erupted in chatter at the sight of two senior partners jostling with each other. After the meeting, I was called into Billy Salomon's office to explain what had happened. I told Billy that if John didn't like what had just happened, all he had to do was stop making snide remarks about me during the weekly briefings. And indeed, the episode put an end to that problem. But tensions between us continued beneath the surface after 1978, when Billy handed the reins to John, who now resented not only what the firm was spending on research but also the fact that I was more the firm's public face than its managing partner.

Although John supported Salomon's incorporation, he did not initiate the move. The path to merger and incorporation actually began quite innocently in May 1981, when my secretary, Helen Katcher, told me that a Mr. Hal Beretz wanted to set up an appointment with me. I had met Hal rather casually once or twice. He was president of Phibro, an NYSE-listed commodities trading house. Coincidentally, his family came from the same small German town of Wenings where I was born. The Beretz family, among the early Jewish settlers in Wenings, had been well known to my parents and grandparents. When Hal Beretz showed up at my office, he was accompanied by David Tendler, the CEO of Phibro.

I assumed the two men wished to chat about general business and financial prospects. Not so. During the commodities boom of the previous decade or so, Phibro had prospered, especially in oil trading. Profitability had been high, and the firm had amassed a large store of capital, quite a bit of it domiciled abroad. Now senior management was looking to diversify their risks. After a long discussion, I suggested they consider taking a position in an insurance company, and I set up an appointment for them with Michael Frinquelli, our firm's senior research analyst on the insurance industry, who was also widely respected for his investment banking knowledge.

Working with our investment banking team, Frinquelli arranged for Phibro to make a bid for NN Corp., a fire and casualty underwriter located in Milwaukee. But Armco Steel outbid Phibro by 50 cents per share. By the time Phibro's deal fell through, senior executives at Phibro and Salomon had gotten to know each other much better. It wasn't long before they were talking about a Phibro–Salomon merger.

Such a merger offered Salomon Brothers at least three major benefits. One was access to capital that would allow the firm to expand its trading and investment banking activities. Second, partners would be able to monetize their capital accounts. (It was a long-standing reality in Wall Street investment banking partnerships that the only way for partners to "cash in" the full value of their partnerships was to "cash out," or leave the firm.) Third, the combination of commodities and securities trading promised to increase business activity in both firms.

I supported the merger, but in hindsight I was wrong. Commodities trading and securities trading are very different beasts. Whereas terms of trade vary widely in the commodities business, they are far more standardized in securities markets. More than that, commodities often originate in undeveloped nations, where laws and norms for conducting business can be lax or infected with corruption, and political instability can inject additional major risk.

Merger negotiations came to consume a lot of my time that summer and fall, and turned out to be extremely stressful. I was drawn into the middle of the deliberations—not merely the financial terms of the deal, but a host of other questions related to Salomon's partners and staff. What incentives were to be given to key employees in order to retain them? Should limited partners be paid off and given some additional annual compensation? Would some general partners be asked to retire? The answer to the last question turned out to be "yes," and somehow it fell to me to sit with John Gutfreund in the meetings with the partners who had to leave the firm.

Some of these meetings remain vivid in my memory. One was with Robert Bernhard, who had been a friend of Gutfreund's since childhood. When the moment arrived, John found it so difficult to tell Robert of his dismissal that he choked up while trying to get the words out. Another was when we dismissed a bright young partner named Michael Bloomberg. In spite of his considerable talents and drive, Bloomberg had not gained traction in the firm largely because of his conflicts with Richard Rosenthal, a senior partner who blocked his career path at Salomon. Bloomberg would open his 1997 autobiography with these paragraphs:

So there I was, thirty-nine years old and essentially hearing, "Here's $10 million; you're history." One summer morning, John

Gutfreund, managing partner of Wall Street's hottest firm, and Henry Kaufman, then the world's most influential economist, told me my life at Salomon Brothers was finished.

"Time for you to leave," said John.

On Saturday, August 1, 1981, I was terminated from the only full-time job I'd ever known and from the high-pressure life I loved. This, after fifteen years of twelve-hour days and six-day weeks.

Out!

Bloomberg—who continues to advise anyone who will listen to see apparent failures as opportunities for even greater success—went on to found a firm so successful it made him one of the ten wealthiest individuals in the world, serve three terms as mayor of New York City, engage in large-scale philanthropy, serve as the UN Secretary General's special envoy for climate action, seriously consider running for president in 2016, and actually do so in 2020.

Another emotional and stressful moment for me was when we met with Bill Salomon to inform him about the merger with Phibro. On a Sunday afternoon, John Gutfreund, Richard Schmeelk, and I flew by helicopter to Bill's summer home in The Hamptons, an affluent region in the South Fork at Long Island's eastern tip. When John informed Bill of the merger, the dialogue was cordial and respectful. But we all understood what was happening. It was a solemn moment—the house of Salomon, a long-standing partnership, was gone. Bill Salomon's lifelong association with a revered family business had come to an end.

Soon after that fateful meeting, at the firm's next Executive Committee meeting, Bill read a letter he had written aloud to the committee's members (and subsequently mailed a personal copy to each of them). The letter made abundantly clear that Bill especially resented not only the sale of the firm but the fact that he had not been consulted about the decision.

> I handed to you, on a gold platter, our name, good will and impeccable reputation. I believed that this great firm would continue the high principles established over so many years and that you would retain the form received as long as possible. And, if any major change was contemplated, it would without question be discussed with me. No, there was no contract or written agreement, just a basic understanding of gentlemen dealing with each other.

In his usual gentlemanly fashion, he added that "though my dreams for the future of Salomon Brothers have been shattered, I will continue to tell the outside world that it is a good deal for the partnership."

My attention to research during those summer months of 1981 suffered. To be sure, the research effort was in the competent hands of skilled analysts and economists. But if I had been paying closer attention to the credit markets, I might have correctly perceived that the secular rise in long-term interest rates was going to peak in October 1981. In turn, I might well have opposed the merger with Phibro, because falling interest rates would have eased the financial pressure on Salomon significantly. And indeed, that's what happened. After the merger was finalized on October 1, trading volume and underwriting climbed, the cost of financing the firm's inventory fell, and profits rose generously. All of that would have put Salomon Brothers in a much stronger position to go public of its own accord rather than turning to a merger partner like Phibro.

Chapter 5

Albert M. Wojnilower, "Dr. Death"

During the same period when I was building a reputation at Salomon Brothers, a fellow economist at First Boston Corporation was sometimes consulted and quoted in the business press: Albert M. Wojnilower. Al and I shared a propensity to go against the tide of upbeat forecasts by regularly injecting cautionary notes into our pronouncements. Just as my often-bearish comments and forecasts inspired many members of the press to dub me "Dr. Gloom," Al Wojnilower was often called "Dr. Death." A May 1981 *Time* magazine story about Wojnilower and me called us "bad news bears," a title that also stuck.* Al and I knew that such colorful labels helped sell newspapers, but these sobriquets nevertheless seemed rather harsh for individuals who were calling the economic trends as they saw them.

Wojnilower built his reputation first and foremost through his brilliant analysis of the linkages between financial and business

---

* In that instance, Wojnilower and I were criticized for going against Reaganomics boosters by issuing warnings about inflationary pressures from tax cuts and increased military spending.

markets, but also through his commitment to objectivity—even if the news was indeed sometimes unwelcome. As with Paul Volcker, Al and I originally overlapped for a time at the New York Fed. And as with Volcker and me, we developed an enduring, valuable friendship. One of the most important Wall Street analysts in the post–World War II period, Albert M. Wojnilower deserves an important place in that history.

Al and I shared some similarities in our backgrounds. He was born in Vienna in 1930, and he and his family fled to America the first week of September 1939—the same week the Nazis invaded Poland. His father, after practicing law in Vienna, now turned to selling insurance. Yet he managed to support the family well enough for Albert (an only child) to attend college. Albert enrolled at Columbia University, and in his second year found his direction while taking his first economics course. Even though Wojnilower graduated class valedictorian in three years and earned a master's degree in economics (also from Columbia) the following year, the placement office did little to help him find work. Suspecting anti-Semitism, he turned for help to a Jewish organization, which arranged a job interview at the Federal Reserve Bank of New York.

In 1951, Wojnilower was hired by the bank's broadminded vice president, Robert Roosa, who oversaw the research department. (Roosa later served as an undersecretary of the US Treasury in the Kennedy and Johnson administrations.) Because of Wojnilower's background and language skills, he was assigned to the bank's Central European Unit, where he focused on Germany. Two years later he moved to the domestic side of research in the bank, where he felt more useful, and remained there for a decade, rising to become chief of the Domestic Research Division.

The same year he joined the New York Fed, Wojnilower entered the PhD program at Columbia, under the direction of the imperious Arthur Burns, who had joined the faculty in 1945. Even though both men were Austrian émigrés to the United States, it was not a close mentoring relationship. The two rarely met, and the student attended none of the professor's classes. Burns was occupied as research director at the National Bureau of Economic Research (1945–1953) and as chair of the US Council of Economic Advisers (1953–1956). Burns later served as the tenth chair of the Federal Reserve. During those years (1970–1978), Wojnilower was largely silent in public about central bank policy, although like many financial economists he expressed public regret when Burns was replaced by banker G. William Miller, as well as some concern about whether Miller could handle the job.

Generously, the New York Fed gave Wojnilower time off to complete his dissertation on credit quality, a topic then of great interest both to the central bank and to the National Bureau of Economic Research. He completed his PhD in 1959.

In 1962, the year I left the New York Fed for Salomon Brothers, Al—also feeling his talents were being underutilized at the central bank—moved to Citibank. We look back on our time at the New York Fed fondly. In the early postwar years, it was an excellent training ground for economists, many of whom went on to build distinguished careers in academics, private finance, or other government service. The building itself, a grand Italian Renaissance–style edifice that by 1935 occupied an entire city

Figure 5.1 The imposing Federal Reserve Bank of New York was an important training ground for economists in the postwar decades. (*Courtesy of The Museum of American Finance, NY, NY*)

block in lower Manhattan's Financial District, conveyed a sense of solidity and power. It was and is the flagship among the Federal Reserve System's branch banks, and holds the world's largest single depository of gold (more than in Fort Knox) in vaults five floors below street level. Those of us who worked there knew it was a major reason New York is the world capital of capital.

After a two-year stint at Citibank, Wojnilower moved to First Boston Corporation, where he would serve as chief economist for twenty-two years.[†] First Boston traced its roots back centuries, to the Massachusetts Bank (1784) and the Safety Fund Bank (1859), later First National Bank of Boston, which merged under the latter's name in 1903. When New Deal banking legislation forced the separation of commercial and investment banking, the firm's investment banking operations were spun off in 1932 as First Boston Corporation. The tenth largest investment bank during World War II, First Boston had by 1950 zoomed up to second place behind Morgan Stanley. That year it was the third largest syndicator in the US, after Halsey Stuart and Morgan Stanley. By the time Wojnilower joined the firm as its chief economist in 1964, First Boston had joined the so-called bulge bracket of top Wall Street investment firms that then included the likes of Morgan Stanley, Kuhn Loeb, and Dillon Read.

Al and I got to know each other better after we both left the New York Fed. He organized a luncheon group that became known as "the Foursome." We got together every few months. There was no set agenda; rather, our conversations unfolded informally over a wide range of topics, although of course the discussions often gravitated to economics, finance, and business. The original members, along with Al and me, were Paul Volcker (during his years at Chase Manhattan Bank) and Leonard J. Santow, who had worked at the Dallas Fed, then had spent much of his career in US government securities at Aubrey G. Lanston & Co., a government securities brokerage house founded in 1949, and then at Griggs & Santow Inc., an investment and economic advisory firm he co-founded with Bill Griggs. Others

---

† First Boston bought a controlling interest in Credit Suisse in 1990, four years after Wojnilower left.

cycled in and out over the years. The foursome disbanded after many years, but Al and I have continued to get together socially and for lunchtime conversation across a wide range of topics, from the personal to the political and economic, including the inevitable reminiscing that comes with age.

Professionally, Al is an economist's economist. Unlike many in the field, he writes extremely well—probably, I imagine, because he invests considerable care in his speeches and prose. For many years, when I was chiefly responsible for putting out *Comments*

Figure 5.2 Albert Wojnilower, circa 1980. *(Courtesy of Albert Wojnilower)*

on Credit at Salomon Brothers, Wojnilower took over the compilation of First Boston's *Handbook of Securities of the United States Government and Federal Agency Securities and Related Money Market Instruments,* which the securities firm published every two years. Because of the distinctive color of the biennial's cover, not to mention its cumbersome title, it was known on Wall Street simply as the "Pink Book." It was chock-full of detailed statistical information and analysis not readily available elsewhere; the twenty-fifth edition (July 1972) ran more than 150 pages.

In the early 1960s, Al and I encountered somewhat different expectations in our new jobs. As noted, I began to regularly turn out reports like *Comments on Credit* and *Prospects for Financial Markets,* whereas the Pink Book appeared every two years. This seemed to suit Wojnilower, who later told an interviewer, "I've never, fortunately, been in the business of having to write something every day or every week or every month." Nor did Al seem temperamentally well-suited for a high public profile, as I found myself drawn into by the late 1960s and early 1970s. More of a loner than I, he enjoyed playing the piano with himself as the only audience. Our writing styles also have differed, with mine tending toward the more direct, while his is a bit more philosophical, elliptical, and nuanced.

Although Al Wojnilower kept a lower profile than I did, by the 1980s he was a highly respected analyst to the point that some journalists made a habit of pairing us as (to quote Vartanig G. Vartan of the *New York Times*) "Wall Street's two most influential economists." Al accomplished this through a combination of the Pink Book's widely recognized value, his insights into both macroeconomic and financial developments as sometimes quoted in the press, his willingness and skill at arguing for unconventional positions in occasional opinion pieces, and his continuing analytical rigor.

That rigor was on full display in an extended academic essay that Al published in a 1980 Brookings Institution economics journal. "The Central Role of Credit Crunches in Recent Financial History" tackled a problem that had been on the minds of financial economists throughout the postwar era as credit crunches periodically plagued the economy.[‡] The forty-nine-page essay, followed by fourteen pages of published expert commentary, stands as a major contribution to the literature of finance and financial history. Wojnilower not only supplied essential data on three decades of US credit data and financial crises, but also offered the unconventional, indeed provocative, interpretation that significant phases of credit expansion have been "essentially supply-determined."

"The key observation, controversial though it may be," Wojnilower argued, "is that the propensity to spend (that is, the demand for nominal GNP) and therefore the demands for credit are inelastic (or at times even perversely positive) with respect to the general level of interest rates." The implications of this finding for policy were enormous; as Wojnilower put it, "At the cyclical level, the chief lesson has been that rationing by interest rate (so-called gradualism) will not stop business expansions." For many Fed officials and so-called Fed watchers, gradualism had become a near religion in recent years. But as someone who also opposed gradualism and carefully tracked

‡   For my analysis of post–World War II credit crunches, see Kaufman, *On Money and Markets*, ch. 13.

supply and demand for credit, I found Al's argument important and convincing.

When he wrote for newspaper readers, Wojnilower also demonstrated a tendency to challenge received wisdom. A few examples illustrate this. In late 1983, readers of the *New York Times* Business Forum pages were greeted by an extended essay titled "The Bogus Issue of the Deficit; Crowding Out U.S. Investment." It was an eye-catching lead; in the early 1980s, as federal budget deficits and the national debt climbed to historic levels, an army of economists—myself among them—warned that the federal government's voracious appetite for credit was "crowding out" corporate borrowing, which in turn was causing private-sector underinvestment and adding inflationary pressure.

To make his case that the worries were misplaced, Wojnilower began by distinguishing between total business investment and net investment (total investment less depreciation), an exercise that revealed a recent shift from longer-term assets (such as buildings) toward shorter-term assets (such as machines). "Since the change probably took place for good reason," he wrote, adding dryly, "I find it hard to get very upset about it." As for the question of whether large deficits hurt economic growth, "it is hard to visualize circumstances in which a larger deficit would not be associated with larger profits and investment than if the deficit were smaller," he wrote. That was especially true in periods of higher unemployment, as in recent years. As for reducing the deficit through spending reductions, Wojnilower saw few viable options. Non-military spending cuts would come at great political cost, and likely would impede economic growth. Cuts in military spending would require a shift in national priorities. In the current environment, he concluded, although the large budget deficit is "undesirable," US economic conditions were being bolstered by a "stampede of foreign investors to buy American Government securities and other assets." In the final analysis, wrote Wojnilower, we need to choose our investments carefully to balance the interests of today and of future generations while not exploiting other nations. "Whether progress toward these goals increases or reduces the budget deficit is immaterial."

The following summer, Wojnilower made a similarly bold claim in a July 18, 1984, *New York Times* op-ed entitled "Stabilize Banking: Restore Some Controls." Today, in the wake of the 2008 financial debacle, such a call hardly seems rebellious. But during President Reagan's first term, deregulation—financial and otherwise—had been fashionable in academics and policy for years, and was only gaining momentum. Still, Wojnilower had a major recent financial calamity to point to: the colossal collapse of the Continental Illinois National Bank and Trust Co. of Chicago a few weeks earlier, which up to then was the largest failure of a financial institution in US history. It was followed by a massive FDIC rescue. Wojnilower worried that without some carefully crafted and targeted banking reregulation—especially the reinstitution of ceilings on interest deposits—similar crises, perhaps followed by a round of regulator overreach, could follow. It was a position I also had been advocating.[§]

In lucid prose, Wojnilower explained the reasons behind deregulation, but also the conundrum it posed for the Fed. "At present, the Federal Reserve Board, with all its expertise,

---

[§]   Henry Kaufman, *The Road to Financial Reformation* (2009), revisits my earlier writings and speeches on this issue.

is striving to support the banking system and to restrain credit expansion at one and the same time. It is an impossible assignment. Until there is a degree of reregulation, both banking problems and inflation are here to stay." Wojnilower concluded by predicting that "The public eventually will react by demanding much more 'hands-on' Government regulation than is needed or desirable. Preventive discipline now would save a great deal of future pain." We now know that more regulation did not follow, while future pain reached a scale no one foresaw.

Wojnilower also challenged conventional wisdom about another pressing economic concern in the 1980s, persistent trade deficits, in "A Long Trade Deficit" (*New York Times*, September 22, 1987). Here again he advocated a more sanguine attitude toward a problem that, when investigated deeply, was nearly intractable and almost certain to persist ("we must learn if not to love our deficit at least to become more relaxed about it."). The chief reason behind obstinate US trade deficits was ongoing globalization, with its continuing regional and national wage disparities and other structural distortions. For that reason, he argued, "In our present strong economy, it would be self-defeating to push for more exports ... [which] would only produce inflation without materially reducing the trade deficit."

Where was Al Wojnilower on the issue of long-term trends in interest rates in the 1970s and into the 1980s? In short, with me. To be sure, we arrived at the position through different methodologies: Al liked to begin his analysis on the economic side and then move to the financial side, whereas I began by looking at the mechanics of credit flows and the feasibility that credit supplies could meet demand, then set those realities within the context of current macroeconomic conditions.

We weren't in touch about the matter, but our distinct pathways led us to the same place at almost exactly the same moment. On Monday, August 16, 1982—the day before the record-breaking day that is the subject of this book—Al Wojnilower also issued a memo that suggested better days ahead for interest rates. Rumors of his changing stance began to circulate through Wall Street, but no news of Wojnilower's memo was reported in the press that day. The next day—the day the markets roared—both the *New York Times* and the *Wall Street Journal* quoted from Wojnilower's memo that "both short-term and long-term interest rates on top-quality obligations will be noticeably lower next year" and "[t]he risks of a flare-up in interest rates have therefore diminished, and the probability of later and lasting declines has been enhanced." The *Journal* also noted Wojnilower's cautionary language—that "for the near term, however, rates remain vulnerable to an upward movement in the business climate." Perhaps the memo's measured language softened its impact. Still, the *Times* story was clear enough that Wojnilower, "one of Wall Street's most influential economists, changed his forecast on interest rates," and concluded that the comments gave the government securities market "a psychological lift."

After market records were shattered August 17, Wojnilower's August 16 memo received more attention and well-deserved credit as having contributed to the bull market. Indeed, on August 18, the *New York Times* published extended excerpts from our two memoranda. At long last, the "bad news bears" had changed their tune.

Kaufman, Wojnilower Statement Excerpts

Following are excerpts from the statements on interest rates issued yesterday by Henry Kaufman, chief economist at Salomon Brothers, and on Monday by Albert M. Wojnilower, chief economist of the First Boston Corporation:

Kaufman

Recent events in the economy and financial markets necessitate a fresh look at the prospects for U.S. interest rates. These events suggest that the present decline in interest rates will continue, although irregularly, with perhaps some dramatic interruptions.

The decline in interest rates and the length of time such a decline will take will largely be determined by both the extent to which the U.S. credit market has been impaired and the level of interest rates that will rejuvenate sustained economic activity. In this context, conventional cyclical benchmarks are no guide. On balance, however, such benchmarks may be the following: long-term U.S. Government bonds now yielding 12¾ percent falling into the 9 percent to 10 percent range within the next 12 months; the Federal funds rate now at 10 percent declining to a low of 6 percent to 7 percent.

A smart recovery in economic activity in the second half of this year is not likely to materialize. This removes the immediate threat to long-term interest rates. Consumer spending, although holding at a high plateau, has failed to respond to tax initiatives, while the rest of the economy is straitjacketed by financial blockages and fear of international competition. Generally poor economic prospects also make businessmen less confident that the economy is able to support substantially higher prices. Thus, [while] inflation expectations are generally eroding, significant economic expansion will require further declines in interest rates and consid-

erable time to unwind major financial impediments.

Wojnilower

The business outlook has deteriorated. The risks of a flare-up in interest rates have therefore diminished, and the prospect of later and lasting declines has been enhanced. Industry sources report, and substantially adverse revisions in June statistical data confirm, that the economic climate turned gloomier toward midyear after having improved during the spring. Capital spending plans were slashed again, and consumption fell, with the result that inventories, particularly of autos but also of materials, resumed piling up at wholesale and retail.

Thus the July 1 tax cut — its immediate cash aspect reduced substantially by niggardly adjustments in withholding schedules — has been more like a life preserver thrown to a struggling swimmer than additional stimulus to an economy already at the point of lift-off.

July performance was little better than June, and gentle improvement will probably be sustained and become more visible in subsequent months. Nevertheless, both the immediate and longer-range outlook have sobered, and this appears to be recognized by the public as well as governmental authorities.

All this reinforces the view that both short- and long-term interest rates on top-quality obligations will be noticeably lower next year.

Chapter 6

Critics, Threats, and Humor

Those who wished I would change my posture had to confront the reality that I continued to be bearishly correct. The response varied from reasoned praise and admiration to frustration and direct criticism. Articles were written about me with titles like "The Wizard of Wall Street" (*New York Times*, May 27, 1979), "Henry Kaufman, America's Interest Rate Guru" (*Institutional Investor*, May 1980), "Kaufman of Salomon Bros.: When Henry Speaks, the World Listens" (*Executive*, August 1980), "How Henry Kaufman Gets It Right" (*Fortune*, May 18, 1981), and "Henry Kaufman, Market Mover" (*Wharton Account*, Winter 1981–1982).

Not all was flattery. After enduring a decade of stagflation, everyone wanted the economy to rebound strongly—especially fans of Reaganomics. On Wall Street, my occasional influence over market movements made some uncomfortable (ironically, even those who may have benefitted by investing in sync with my forecasts). It seemed that some investors, getting the cause and effect relationship backward, were holding me responsible for bad financial and economic news. "If only Henry would change his tune," they seemed to think, "everything will be fine." The tune I was singing was because much was *not* fine.

At the *New York Post*, the city's colorful and irreverent paper designed for those without the patience to wade through one of the more substantial papers, Maxwell Newton was making a sport of criticizing me—indeed, he seems to have coined the Dr. Doom label. Newton, an Australian, had enjoyed some success in business newspaper publishing in the 1960s, then moved into Marvel comic book reprints in 1975, which failed financially. He emigrated to the US, taking up the job as financial editor at the *Post*, which was owned by fellow far-right conservative Australian Rupert Murdoch. As we will see in chapter seven, Newton almost rabidly supported Reaganomics, and so was a harsh critic of anyone who didn't share his enthusiasm.

Attacks on me reached an extreme when I began to receive death threats. In the late 1970s, I received a call from an FBI agent with concerns about my safety. During a raid on the premises of a Puerto Rican terrorist, the Bureau had found a list with the names of twenty apparent targets—my name among them. Possibly I was targeted because Salomon may have underwritten some Puerto Rican borrowings. The FBI had few leads, so the agent left his name and number along with some advice: I should drive a different route to work each day. And, while walking down the street, I should walk in the middle of the sidewalk. None of this seemed especially reassuring.

Around the same time, someone from the Chicago trading pits phoned Salomon Brothers and threatened: "We are going to get Henry." And another threatening call came from an irate institutional investor. Salomon Brothers assigned a driver to me as well as a bodyguard who was supposed to accompany me everywhere. The first evening, my wife Elaine and I didn't want the fellow sleeping outside in his car all night, so we invited him in to sit on our living room couch. Later that night, one of our sons was startled to come upon the bodyguard sleeping in our living room, with two handguns in his open briefcase.

I had never imagined the job of analyzing bond markets and forecasting interest rates could be filled with such drama. But after about a week, I dismissed the bodyguard as too much of an intrusion in our lives. I wanted to get back to normal life, although I kept the car and driver, which allowed me to work while commuting. As for walking down the center of the side-walk, half a century later the habit remains with me.

Along with critics of my forecasts—reasonable and otherwise—my growing influence often attracted satire. Comedy can be a wonderful outlet for expressing such anxieties but also for simply poking some fun at celebrities. This was hardly surprising, and indeed I enjoyed the parodies. Here, after all, was a rather short-in-stature, balding, middle-aged economist who lived an unostentatious lifestyle compared with many similarly compensated Wall Streeters. Poring over reams of dry data, I figured out—through a process mysterious to most, and so seemingly magical!—which way the winds of economic change were likely to blow. These were great elements for parody.

The New York Financial Writers Association made my unwitting fame as an economist the theme of their 1982 production of the Financial Follies, called "How Lovely to Be Famous." I was played by a McGraw-Hill editor named Robert Kozma, who dressed as Merlin the magician. Here are the first few stanzas, sung to the theme of the Major General's Song in Gilbert and Sullivan's *Pirates of Penzance*:

KAUFMAN:

I am the very model of a modern-day economist,

I specialize in frightening news and predications ominous;

I've studied all important thought and all the schools eponymous,

From Marxian to Keynesian, as well as those anonymous;

I postulate my theories with a marvelous lucidity,

Explaining every aspect of the law of disutility;

I have a lot of brilliant views on monetary symmetry,

With many cheerful facts about the crisis of liquidity.

ALL:

With many cheerful facts about the crisis of liquidity,

With many cheerful facts about the crisis of liquidity,

With many cheerful facts about the crisis of liquidity.

KAUFMAN:

I know precisely how to do a quartile deviation, or,

To tell exactly what the word "disintermediation"'s for;

In short, in matters frightening and predications ominous,

I am the very model of a modern-day economist.

ALL
In short, in matters frightening and predications ominous,
He is the very model of a modern-day economist.

As *American Banker* accurately reported, the night of that performance, "the member of the audience most convulsed with laughter was Henry Kaufman."

Pulitzer Prize–winning journalist and satirist Russell Baker, also a columnist for the *New York Times* from 1962 to 1998, got into the act with a piece of dry humor about my influence. In his signature self-deprecating style, Baker confessed to a "lifelong struggle to become Ben Bolt," the protagonist in an 1843 poem of the same name written by Thomas Dunn English. In the poem, "Sweet Alice . . . wept with delight . . . when [Bolt] gave [her] a smile / And trembled with fear at [his] frown." I had become "the Ben Bolt of Wall Street," Baker explained—a status not without its apprehensions. "Kaufman probably never indulges in gloom for the pure sport of it," the satirist speculated, which "must take a fearful amount of self-control." Perhaps stockbrokers lingered outside my window at night to catch a glimpse of my mood, Baker wondered, or maybe my easy chair was bugged. The piece, titled "Ben Bolt is in the Street," was reprinted in *Institutional Investor* under the title "Poor Henry Kaufman."

Some journalists had fun exaggerating even more by portraying me as a near deity. Here are a few passages from "A Life in the Day of Henry Kaufman," a send-up in *Province* magazine by columnist Eric Nicol:

I rise early, wakened by a beam of light from heaven that shines directly, but with respect, into my eyes.

OBSERVER

Ben Bolt Is in The Street

By Russell Baker

Reading about the boom on Wall Street last week brought to mind the poem about sweet Alice and Ben Bolt, which begins, "Don't you remember sweet Alice, Ben Bolt . . .?"

Out of deference to poetry lovers, I'll forgo a full recitation. It's enough to say that Ben Bolt had such power over Alice that she melted with joy when he smiled and trembled with fear at his frown.

Since first encountering this chestnut in childhood, I have always wanted to be one of the world's Ben Bolts, with power to make creatures of both sexes respond obediently to my moods. Unfortunately, life hasn't worked out that way, but never mind that right now; I want to get on to Henry Kaufman, who has apparently succeeded where I have failed.

Most of the explanations I saw for Wall Street's big spree gave credit to — among other things — Henry Kaufman's optimism. Mr. Kaufman, I gathered, is the Ben Bolt of Wall Street.

For months he had been frowning and the stock market trembled with fear. Then about a week ago — if I am reading the stories right — he awoke with a smile and the market melted with joy.

For those like me who shun the stock market as they do the dice tables at Las Vegas and the three-card monte games in Times Square, I should explain that Mr. Kaufman is an economist for a big financial house in Wall Street. Unlike Washington economists, who are regarded as little better than carnival barkers for politicians, Wall Street economists are taken seriously by the stock market crowd, and none is taken more seriously than Mr. Kaufman. "When Henry is gloomy, the market despairs; when Henry smiles, the whole street smiles with him," they say at the stock exchange.

Mr. Kaufman's success in achieving the power of Ben Bolt makes me wonder for the first time if it's all it's cracked up to be. I'm not sure I'd want the stock market taking a tailspin every time I happened to be feeling gloomy about the future, which happens to be the way I feel a lot of the time.

You'd probably have stock brokers peeping at your window late at night to see whether you looked like the soul of gaiety in the living room or whether you were just sitting there brooding into your snifter over man's inescapable mortality.

Suppose, pouring the second brandy too many, you said to your wife, "What difference does it make in the long run whether Union Carbide goes up ⅞ or loses ¼ tomorrow?" The sharp operators would probably have your easy chair bugged, and next day — thud — it would be goodbye stock market.

Well, of course Mr. Kaufman probably never indulges himself in gloom for the pure sport of it, the way most people do. I imagine he refuses ever to wallow in a bout of gloom unless all the market indicators have given him clearance. This is probably why his pessimism and his optimism, too, are so closely watched by the money people.

They probably say, "You can count on Henry never to mope for the pure fun of it." I respect him for that, but it must take a fearful amount of self-control. What does he do when he comes home evenings in the mood for a pleasant wallow in gloomy self-pity, and all the market indicators are giving him the smile signal?

If he's like most of us, he wants everybody to make a fuss over him and say, "Cheer up, Henry, you're the sweetest, most wonderful guy in the world and we all love you." But you can't enjoy the pleasure of having everybody try to cheer you up if you're the Ben Bolt of Wall Street, can you? Chances are your wife and children, seeing you come home looking glum, will abandon you and head for the telephones to place sell orders with their brokers.

My lifelong struggle to become Ben Bolt has had results of a very different kind. For many years now I have been

The market melted at Kaufman's smile

an infallible indicator of what not to do in the marketplace. Upon hearing that I approve of a television show, the networks immediately cancel it. If I applaud a movie, it disappears from theaters next day and is never heard of again.

When I recommend a book, it is a signal to everyone in the community not to buy it. And if, after searching through 8,000 breakfast cereals, I finally find a good one and return to the grocer for a second box, he says, "They've quit making that one."

This is the opposite of being Ben Bolt: when I smile in the marketplace, whole corporations tremble with fear. But it doesn't work if I try to fake the smile so as to destroy some monstrosity I detest. The market can tell that my smile is fake and the monstrosity sells millions, just as the market can tell when my smile is genuine and recognize when there is something abroad in the land that must be stamped out.

As you can see, I am already embarked on a pleasant journey into self-pity and gloom. Poor Henry Kaufman can't do that.

Figure 6.1 (From The New York Times. © 1982 The New York Times Company. All rights reserved. Used under license. www.nytimes.com)

I go to the bathroom like other mortals. Except of course that when I flush the toilet it activates 2,700 computers in the stock exchanges of the world.

I breakfast simply—a little milk and honey, with pomegranates, or myrrh and aloes with all the chief spices. My breath alone is enough to raise AT&T ten points . . .

Duly and with the day yet dawning I come to the Wall Street offices of Salomon Brothers. The doorman . . . shields his eyes against the wondrous light of my ascending without using the elevator.

Should I appear pessimistic, the word spreads quickly and in a matter of minutes there is an increase in the rate of suicide among stock brokers. It distresses me to think of them standing on 30-storey [*sic*] window ledges, waiting for me to frown.

Sidney Rutberg of the *Daily News Record* created dialogue between a dad and his confused (about economics) son to explain the August 17 boom to readers.

Hey Dad, I hate to bug you again, but you've got to tell me what happened in the stock market last week. I hear prices went through the roof one day, and the next day, the market traded 132 million shares.

It's very simple, son. Two of Wall Street's big name economists—a fellow named Henry Kaufman of Salomon Brothers and another guy with a really big name, Albert Wojnilower of First Boston—said business was lousier than they expected it to be and the chances of a good recovery were getting dimmer.

Come off it, Dad. Are you trying to say that bad news like that can push stock prices way up?

To my surprise, I was also portrayed in at least one novel. The author was Michael M. Thomas, a former partner at Lehman Brothers (and son of a prominent Wall Streeter) who left the investment world for a second career as a novelist and sometimes essayist. Writing about what he knew best, Thomas specialized in financial thrillers. *Someone Else's Money*, published in 1982, was his second of nine novels. I make a few appearances as a character known on Wall Street as the Merchant of Misery. At one point, a key character finds that "the worst was yet to come [in the form of] the blow from the Merchant of Misery which would fall on Friday morning." The blow came in the form of Merchant's predictions at a prominent economic forum in New York that the federal deficits in the next two years were likely to reach $100 billion to $125 billion, with the prime rate climbing as high as 22 percent. The figures could have come right out of one of my contemporary speeches about Reaganomics.

I recall having lunch with Mr. Thomas around that time, and I assume he drew on his impressions of me across the table to help fill in gaps for his fictional characterization:

The Street's mind pictured the Merchant of Misery as squat homunculus who dwelt in a moldy cellar amid lizards and snakes and retorts bubbling with noxious evil potions; he was in fact a short, intelligent, middle-aged man, with a pleasant, mild face and a disagreeable tendency to stick with the possible facts when all about him were spouting concepts. "There is nothing wrong per se with being optimistic," he was fond of saying, "but it is also not a moral necessity."

In the novel, the speech is reported in the press and casts a pall over Wall Street. "His verbal elegance drew slim appreciation from a financial community doomed to pass a rainy, muggy weekend licking its wounds and pondering its desperate future." Whichever month in 1982 the novel was released, Mr. Thomas seems likely to have sent it to press before August.

Cartoons published in magazines and newspapers were one of my favorite forms of humor and satire, especially when about me. The pages that follow include cartoons published about me in a variety of outlets. Like the writers just described, cartoonists typically poked fun at my alleged gloominess and my reputation and influence in Wall Street. The cartoons in this sampling were published before and after the flood of press coverage following August 17, 1982. Cartoons published specifically about my role in that record day are reproduced at the end of chapter two.

"*His name is Henry Kaufman and God knows he's gloomy,
but he's not the gloomy Henry Kaufman.*"

CartoonCollections.com

Figure 6.2 The "Dr. Gloom" label became so embedded, at least in New York circles, that *The New Yorker* knew its readers would "get" this cartoon. *(Lorenz Lee/Cartoon Collections)*

Figure 6.3 Sophisticated readers also understood some of the perils of making financial forecasts, as *The Cape Codder* in Massachusetts quipped about. *(Courtesy The Cape Codder)*

Figure 6.4 *(Credit: Doris Ettlinger)*

Figure 6.5 Perhaps because of my ethnicity, not to mention Germany's economic stature, newspapers there covered me closely. The English-language cartoon below appeared in a German-language newspaper. *(Michael Cummings / MirrorPix)*

"Well, my adviser is H. Kaufman, and when H. Kaufman talks, everybody STAMPEDES!"

Figure 6.6 The New York Post demonstrated its signature flamboyant style with this cartoon published the day after the rally. The stampede is a long-standing theme in Wall Street history. New York Post, August 19, 1982. (Paul Rigby/New York Post)

'How Lovely to Be Famous'

KAUFMAN:
I am the very model of a modern-day economist,
I specialize in frightening news and predications ominous;
I've studied all important thought and all the schools eponymous,
From Marxian to Keynesian, as well as those anonymous;
I postulate my theories with a marvelous lucidity,
Explaining every aspect of the law of disutility;
I have a lot of brilliant views on monetary symmetry,
With many cheerful facts about the crisis of liquidity.

ALL:
With many cheerful facts about the crisis of liquidity,
With many cheerful facts about the crisis of liquidity,
With many cheerful facts about the crisis of liquidity.

Figure 6.7 I was featured in the arts in some rather unconventional ways—as when an Annapolis, Maryland, movie theater spelled out "Henry Kaufman, We Love You" on their marquee and when the Financial Follies build their show around me (as a Merlin-like wizard). *(Financial Follies 1982 lyrics by Jefferson Grigsby, Courtesy NYFWA)*

Contemplating the current stampede for shares on the world's stock markets, Eric Nicol hears the voice of the oracle who triggered it all by saying that interest rates have finally cracked — Henry Kaufman, chief economist for the Wall Street firm of Salomon Brothers.

A LIFE IN THE DAY OF

HENRY KAUFMAN

"I rise early, wakened by a beam of light from heaven that shines directly, but with respect, into my eyes.

"I go to the bathroom like other mortals. Except of course that when I flush the toilet it activates 2,700 computers in the stock exchanges of the world.

"I breakfast simply — a little milk and honey, with pomegranates, or myrrh and aloes with all the chief spices. My breath alone is enough to raise AT&T 10 points. My garb befits my station as the economist's economist: the cloth of the prophet, gathered together in solemn communion with my limbs. If I favor black as the color of my garment, it is because the black is what the good investor prays to be in. The red I reserve for the privacy of my undershorts.

"After my matinal repast I walk to work, across the East River, using the bridge only if the water is frozen and

Marv Newland

Figure 6.8 My influence inspired a variety of creative satires, including one that portrayed me as a deity and another in which a father tries to explain how bad news can make stocks rise. *(Marv Newland/The Province)*

Chapter 7

Growing Pressures

With the Phibro-Salomon merger completed in fall 1981, I resumed devoting all my time to analyzing markets, overseeing research, meeting with important clients, and speaking with members of the press. As the new year approached, I continued to hold my long-standing bearish position on markets and to issue cautionary forecasts. I did not anticipate the new year to be especially eventful, but as it turned out, the first six months of 1982 were an especially trying time for me professionally.

Even though I had never declared a political party affiliation, top members of the Reagan administration came to regard me as a devoted critic of their macroeconomic policies. They were joined by a few strongly conservative members of the business press who harshly criticized some of my forecasts. As pressure to conform to the emerging doctrine of supply-side economics grew, some editorialists wondered whether I had "lost my touch." As the months of early 1982 ticked by, I began to feel as if my reputation was on the line.

The stakes were also getting higher because my influence on market movements continued to grow. And indeed, the new

year opened with just such an example. On the first Monday of
the new year, I shared the major findings of our 1982 edition
of *Prospects for Financial Markets*. As the *Wall Street Journal*
reported, "Mr. Kaufman warned that 'a confrontation between
the credit needs of the US Treasury and those of business corporations is shaping up in 1982' and that interest rates 'will start to
trend irregularly upward again before midyear' and by year end
long-term interest rates 'will probably be threatening their 1981
highs.'" When we shared the report at a press conference the
next day, its major findings—combined with unexpected news
that day that the Fed had increased the money supply—drove
down stock prices 17.22 points (to 865.30), or 2 percent. It was
the largest one-day decline in four months. Stocks on the Tokyo
exchange also plummeted Tuesday.

Several observers pointed out that "dealers . . . were aware
of what Mr. Kaufman would say before he issued his annual
forecast" (*New York Times*), and the American Bankers Association's *Banking Journal* reminded its readers that I had been
warning about exploding debt for the last twenty years. Even so,
financial reporting on the slump in stock prices roundly ascribed
it to my Monday–Tuesday forecasts, from the *Washington Post*,
the always colorful *New York Post* ("Stocks Dive After Kaufman
Forecast" and "Kaufman Helps Put Market in Tailspin") and
other East Coast papers, to the other coast's *Los Angeles Times*
and *Los Angeles Herald Examiner* ("Dr. Doom: We're on a
Credit Collision Course").

In the nation's heartland, Indiana's *Evansville Press* used the
early 1982 rout as an occasion to reflect upon my market influence. I had long predicted high interest rates, the paper reminded

its readers, and "what he said rippled through the stock and bond markets slowly and lastingly. He was painfully correct over the long run." More recently, the article continued, "both the bond and stock markets rebounded in the fall after Kaufman modified his stance on interest rates increasing to new records." On a more personal note, the author noted that I was "widely respected" without being "flamboyant"—high praise in the sensible Midwest.

A sub theme ran through press coverage of the January 4 bear market, one that became more and more pronounced as the year unfolded: I was categorized as a leading critic of Reaganomics. This was misleading. To begin with, I had never been affiliated with a political party nor professed to be a Democrat or Republican. Nor was I opposed to the Reagan administration's economic policies in toto. President Reagan generally didn't interfere with monetary policy; his primary aspiration was to hold down the deficit. Rather, I was gravely concerned with the budgetary consequences—namely, skyrocketing debt—that resulted from a combination of President Reagan's policies: the deep tax cuts, the increased military spending, and the failure (with Congress) to rein in rising social welfare spending. But as the core issue of rising deficits and debt became more prominent in business and economic circles in the early 1980s, those who expressed clear positions on the matter were inevitably politicized.

Early in 1982, the pressure was getting higher on the Reagan administration. As a writer for the influential *Journal of Commerce* explained on January 11, "Over the next week or so President Reagan will make some of the most critical decisions of his presidency in setting forth the broad outline of government expenditures for 1983 and beyond. This will be the president's first budget starting from scratch and it will set the tone for subsequent budget decisions in his administration."

I was far from alone in voicing concerns about the risks of rising government debt crowding out private borrowing. Indeed, on that specific point and some others related to Reaganomics, many investors and economists shared my views. The *Chicago Tribune* observed that "most of the economic profession does not believe Reagan's program will work"; indeed, the esteemed MIT economist Robert Solow made the same point before Reagan was elected when speaking as president of the American Economic Association but also on behalf of the vast majority of AEA members. As Karen W. Arenson of the *New York Times* (writing for the *International Herald Tribune*) noted astutely, because of my "mystique" on Wall Street, I became a kind of avatar for broad criticism of Reaganomics, "as though [Kaufman] were personally responsible for the financial markets' deep-seated skepticism toward the Reagan program."

This oversimplification was memorialized in a growing number of press reports. *Forbes* dubbed me a "supply-side critic." London's *Economist* coined "Kaufmania" as a shorthand for opposition to Reaganomics. The *Chicago Tribune* claimed I was "making a career as a Reaganomics critic." In a major essay for *Barron's*, "Credit and Creditability: Henry Kaufman v. Supply-Side Economics," Peter Brimelow asserted that my forecast record the previous year had been mixed and criticized me for my alleged "deviation from classical economics." Similarly, *Forbes* concluded that I and other supply-side critics did not understand the benefits of the new orthodoxy—that we "don't consider the shot in the arm that corporate cash flow will get

from lower income taxes and from greatly liberalized depreciation allowances." Striking a more tongue-in-cheek tone, the
Journal of Commerce claimed there was "only one way out of
this recession, depression, repression or whatever. President Reagan has to persuade, convince, subvert, co-opt, or inveigle Henry
Kaufman. We would have added intimidate but we don't think
that possible."

Key members of the Reagan administration began to take aim
at me as well. Reacting to my 1982 forecasts, Murray L. Weidenbaum, chairman of the Council of Economic Advisers, scoffed that
I was "recycling [my] forecast for 1981." Revealingly, Weidenbaum was evasive about the possibility of deficit-ameliorating
tax hikes, and by March was admitting that the administration
had to "scale down its recovery estimates and to raise its deficit
projections." For his part, US Treasury Secretary Donald Regan
"rushed to network TV to issue a sharp dissent" to our 1982
edition of *Prospects* (as *Barron's* reported), and "disagreed stren-
uously with the Salomon economist, saying that rates in 1982
will come down." Yet he too hinted that some sort of tax hike
might be warranted in the future. As the weeks passed, Regan
grew increasingly frustrated by the reluctance of many Wall
Streeters—with me as the lightning rod—to "believe" in the
wonders of Reaganomics. But by July, when unemployment was
still a punishing 9.5 percent, the Treasury secretary was forced
to admit that his sunny early-1982 assertions that the economy
would be "roaring" by February were "a little bit of hyperbole."

The administration's young wunderkind budget director,
David Stockman, had a more complicated relationship with
Reaganomics, and therefore with my pronouncements. As those

who lived through the eventful early 1980s will recall, Stockman, one of the main architects of Reaganomics, grew to challenge some of its fundamentals. A few weeks earlier (December 1981), Stockman had given a long interview with William Greider for the *Atlantic Monthly* ("The Education of David Stockman") in which he admitted that the Reagan tax cuts were a "Trojan horse to bring down the top rate . . . It's kind of hard to sell 'trickle down,'" and further that "none of us really understands what's going on with all these numbers." Already losing influence within the administration, Stockman reportedly began to shift his fiscal position based in part on my warnings about budget shortfalls, while still generally toeing the Reaganomics line. (He resigned from the Office of Management and Budget in 1985.)

Not surprisingly, Maxwell Newton of the *New York Post* (see previous chapter) carried the faulty Kaufman v. Reaganomics trope to extremes. The paper normally reported on me in a rather straightforward way—except when the byline was Newton's, and especially when the topic was supply-side economics. Not satisfied with labeling me (variously) Dr. Doom or Dr. Death, in early 1982 Newton went on to identify the "Gang of 6 Ambushing Reagan": Al Wojnilower and me, Jude Wanniski, David Stockman, Lawrence Kudlow (then serving under Stockman at OMB), and Fed Chairman Paul Volcker—all of us allegedly supported by "the whole left-liberal power structure in press, radio, and television." A couple of months after that, Newton fretted about what he called the "Undercover Socialists of America," this time led by Al Wojnilower and me along with Speaker of the House Thomas P. "Tip" O'Neill. Such ravings were far out of the mainstream of economic and financial commentary, arguably even on the pages of a newspaper owned by conservative publishing magnate Rupert Murdoch. Still, Newton seemed to enjoy his platform, which he used to make his own economic predictions while frequently challenging mine. Following the bear market I caused in early January, Newton threw down the gauntlet: "It is now apparent that 1982 is the year when the reputation of Henry Kaufman will face the final test."

As the months rolled by, I had to admit that some others were of the same mind. My bearish stance on interest rates and ballooning government debt was becoming increasingly unpopular among analysts and investors eager for a return to prosperous times. When bond traders met that May in Boston, most of those polled expressed agreement with my view that long periods with a positive yield curve were unlikely, yet most were adding to their bond portfolios. *Bondweek*'s story about the gathering was titled "Portfolio Managers to Henry K.: 'You're Wrong.'"

Speculation that I was losing my touch even infected some of the satire about me. The same month as the *Bondweek* article, *Euromoney* published a humorous skit about a Mafia don in the "olive oil business" who asks his board members to tell him about "the real big cheeses." They explain that "there's a guest speaker coming in from New York, boss, called Doctor Henry Kaufman."

Don Vito was puzzled. "What's with this doctor bit? In our business we don't take no prisoners so we don't need no medics."

"Let me explain," said Giulio. "He's not a real doctor. He's a sort of fortune-teller who made a big name for himself in 1979–1980, reading palms and tea leaves, but recently he's been slipping. New folks don't turn up in droves to listen to him anymore in New York, so they ship him 3,000 miles to Europe, where they don't complain if his star-gazing is way out of line."

Believing it wrong to bow to such pressure, I not only remained bearish about interest rates throughout the spring, I also spoke out about other troubling indicators revealed by our analysis. Along with the president's lax fiscal policy, I was becoming increasingly alarmed by the administration's overreliance on monetarism. As I explained to a writer for *Dun's Business Month* in May 1982, the current practice of targeting the money supply was inflicting "unacceptable economic and financial violence" on the economy. "Under monetarism," I went on, "there are no restraints other than those produced by interest rates," which causes gyrating interest rates and other problems. My advice to the Fed was to target the growth of credit instead of the money supply. Somewhat painfully, this position was at odds with Fed policy under the chairmanship of my old friend and colleague, Paul Volcker. Although not a monetarist, Volcker felt compelled to embrace the policy for a while in order to raise interest rates sharply and in turn drive down inflation.

In March I had been widely quoted in the international business press for warning that "I have never seen business's financial situation as fragile as it is today." Three months later, I similarly warned that "[o]ur economy and financial markets are more fragile than they have been at any time since the end of World War II." Did that mean a recession was inevitable? Hardly, as I explained to the *U.S. News & World Report*: "Twenty years ago I would have said the odds were 1,000 to 1 against another depression; 10 years ago, 100 to 1 against it; today, the odds are maybe 8 or 10 to 1. That is still substantially against it, but the odds are coming down." One action that could help, I proposed, was to reduce the Reagan tax cuts from 10 percent to 5 percent, which of course miffed Reagan loyalists. The fact was, in that same interview I criticized aspects of both Republican and Democratic economic policy.

In spite of scattered speculation that I was "slipping," a strong majority of Wall Street watchers continued to regard me as "mild-mannered," objective, "not partisan," and someone who "keeps predicting things that turn out to be more or less accurate." And for that reason, I remained someone to be reckoned with. As Wade McGowan of Chase Manhattan Bank observed in July 1982, "You can't afford not to follow him. Believe him or not, the root fact is, when he speaks, the market does a number, whether it's the futures, cash or stock market." The point was driven home on July 12, when one of my comments squelched a bond rally and caused traders to "run for cover."

Later that month (July 23), the New York *Daily News* reported, "Rumors that super bear economist Henry Kaufman has turned bullish on interest rates jolted a sleepy stock market in the plus column late in the session yesterday on the New York Stock Exchange. But when the reports couldn't be confirmed, stocks shaded their best gains." This barely-noticed incident would prove to be the harbinger of something much larger to come. But neither Wall Street watchers nor I myself predicted it about three weeks later.

It was around that time that my wife, Elaine, and I flew to Europe for a much-needed two-week vacation. I had been traveling a lot for business in Europe and Asia, living out of a suitcase, so I wanted to relax rather than tour actively on this trip.

We spent most of our time unwinding on Madeira, a tiny island off the coast of Portugal. Alas, I found it nearly impossible to relax, even when swimming in the sparkling sea. I couldn't get work, especially the interest rate picture, out of my mind. I kept ruminating about my outlook for the financial markets. I kept checking daily updates on market and economic activity from my office back in Manhattan. During our vacation and through the week after we returned home, the Salomon Brothers *Bond Market Roundup* began with these passages:

July 16, 1982: "The bond market staged another rally based on a lower Federal funds rate and speculation that the Federal Reserve

Figure 7.1 As my wife, Elaine, and I vacationed in Madeira, Portugal, I was preoccupied with interest rate analysis. (Walter Rudolph/ United Archives/Universal Images Group via Getty Images)

is easing its credit policy. The Federal funds rate fell to 12.75% on Friday—a reduction of 175 basis points in just two weeks."

July 23, 1982: "The bond market continued to post gains for the fourth consecutive week fueled by the confirmation that Fed policy had been eased. The Government yield curve became much more positive, 238 basis points, on the strength of the 127 basis points decline in bill rates."

July 30, 1982: "A reduction in the discount rate to 11%, an $800 million decline in money supply and the lowering of the prime rate to 15% at a few banks transformed a losing week to a winner."

August 6, 1982: "The bond market was mixed this week showing modest price increases in municipal issues, while taxables were fractionally lower."

August 13, 1982: "Economic news, showing little if any rebound from June and an accommodative Federal Reserve, including a half-point cut in the discount rate to 10½% last Friday, gave all sectors of the bond market a boost this week. The Treasury yield curve continued to widen to 338 basis points and is now more positive than ever before."

Once back in the office, I spoke with a number of bond traders to get a feel for the current market. Then, on Saturday, August 14, I sequestered myself in my study to delve back into the most recent data on bond prices and rates and other indexes on financial and economic performance. But I also thought deeply about the bigger picture, about the structure of financial markets.

At this critical moment in my professional life, as during several others before, I recalled sage advice that Sidney Homer offered me. "Henry," he had remarked after hiring me as a bond market researcher at Salomon Brothers in 1962, "someday you will be asked to make forecasts on prospects in the financial markets. In doing so, you may find it helpful to begin with a historical perspective and evaluate the importance of the structural changes in the marketplace before you reach a conclusion on market prospects."

A month or so after his comment, I had come to understand what he meant by historical perspective. He had just finished writing a book called *A History of Interest Rates from 1000 B.C. to the Present*. Handing one copy of the page proofs to me and another to my secretary, he asked me to read the 594-page tome aloud in order to catch errors or awkward language. So I did—including every figure in all eighty-two interest rate tables. Sidney's inscription of my copy read: "To Henry Kaufman, who is the only man alive who ever has and ever will read this book out loud." I learned from that exercise that reading aloud is an excellent way to improve one's writing. More importantly, I came to see patterns in the historical evolution of bond markets that have remained with me for many decades.

So as I once again considered secular and cyclical trends in interest rates two decades later, I discerned an important pattern. The secular patterns that Sidney had charted in his book stretch out over long periods, often many decades, when interest rates sweep upward or downward. Although these broad movements often are interrupted by cyclical fluctuations lasting from less than a year to several years, they are nevertheless identifiable. The data showed that the American bond market had experienced the longest yield upswing in history. The climb had persisted for some thirty-five years, through October 1981, raising long-term yields 454 percent in the process.

When it came to cyclical trends—a subject I had pursued closely—several facts were indisputable. Since 1948–1950, the long, relentless rise in yields had encompassed six cyclical bear markets and six cyclical bull markets with, of course, the magnitude of the cyclical upswing in interest rates larger than the downswing. At the same time, I could see that the yield on three-month US Treasury bills had reached 17 percent on a bond equivalent basis, but had peaked at 15 percent in October 1981, and now stood at 10 percent.

As I scrutinized recent events, several developments stood out. First, the American economy was losing its vitality. Industrial production was dropping. New housing activity was stalling, and consumers were losing spending power. And there were even more signs of economic deterioration. In July, the unemployment rate rose to 9.8 percent, a new postwar peak. In the financial markets, there was a noticeable rise in bank failures and other mishaps. Drysdale Government Securities, a modest-sized firm, had collapsed in May. The next month, a small bank in Oklahoma named Penn Square became insolvent because its financing was highly concentrated in oil and gas, and it had sold participation in these loans to other banks—including to prominent money-center banks.

On the broader domestic stage, I was well aware of the tough monetary policies Paul Volcker had been pursuing at the Fed in an effort to wring chronic inflation out of the US economy. Thanks to Volcker's steadiness and persistence, executives at major financial institutions were finally learning to slow their excessive lending and investing, and no longer assumed that high inflation was baked into the economy.

As for the international scene, Argentina had devalued its currency. In Europe, Banco Ambrosiano, a subsidiary of a Luxembourg subsidiary, went into default. Because Ambrosiano was linked through transactions to many prominent European and American banks, its collapse cast a wide shadow.

Thus, as I took into account contemporary, recent, and historical data and institutional developments, domestic as well as international, I was moved to conclude that the economic exuberance generated by the interplay between business and finance was diminishing rapidly. Bond interest rates already had begun to fall, and I now believed their decline was not a short-term cyclical movement but rather the start of a long secular decline. As rates fell, of course, bond prices would rise. The time had arrived for me to shed my bearishness about the bond market.

Knowing that this announcement likely would attract some attention, I spent the rest of the weekend and into Monday carefully crafting a memo that laid out my new position and the reasoning behind it. With some additions here and deletions there, I was finally satisfied with the handwritten memo by Monday evening.

Part III

The Aftermath

Chapter 8

Other Record Days on Wall Street

During the Gilded Age of the late nineteenth century, colorful speculators such as Jay Gould, "Jubilee Jim" Fisk, and Daniel Drew manipulated, cornered, and otherwise toyed with stock markets for personal gain in ways that eventually were made illegal by insider trading and other securities laws. Another cohort of "high rollers" helped boost 1920s Wall Street to historic heights before its infamous crash in the fall of 1929. With a wave of securities trading reforms under President Franklin Roosevelt's New Deal and the relative quiescence of trading during depression and world war, Wall Street emerged in the postwar period as a respectable and increasingly accessible venue for upper- and middle-class investment.

Throughout the second half of the twentieth century, financial markets, with only mild, short-term fluctuations, climbed steadily, interrupted only by the stagnant 1970s. Single-day downward or upward swings seldom exceeded 5 percent. That changed as the twenty-first century ushered in three especially turbulent periods (so far): the dot-com boom and bust (1995–2002), the subprime mortgage crisis (2007–2009), and the current coronavirus pandemic.

Table 8.1 lists all the days since the Second World War when the Dow closed up as much (4.8 percent) or more than the historic day that is the story of this book. The business press covered each of those bull markets. Taken together, this evidence shows that no private citizen in the modern history of Wall Street has caused a one-day bull market comparable to August 17, 1982.

Consider the days with one-day surges of 5 percent or more. The first instance (May 27, 1970) was typical of many large single-day gains. As the *New York Times* put it the next day, "There was no specific news to trigger the rally." Often, one-day bull markets are nestled within a series of similar (though not quite as dramatic) trading days as markets reverse previous multi-day downward trends. As the *Times* went on to say of this spring day in 1970, "Many Wall Street analysts were inclined to view the recovery as essentially technical in nature, a normal rebound from the heavy pounding that stocks have taken in the last week."

A full seventeen years passed before the bulls raged again on a comparable scale. But again, what made October 20, 1987, exceptional was not the actions of an individual but rather a collective shift among investors who had been battered for several previous days. The day before—Black Monday—the Dow had fallen 508 points, or 22.6 percent, the largest one-day decline in Wall Street history. As the *Wall Street Journal* reported on October 21, "Yesterday was the first advance after four wrenching sessions where the average lost 769.74 points." It wasn't

Single-Day U.S. Bull Markets, 1945-2019	
(S&P 500 gains > 4.7 percent)	
May 27, 1970	5.0
August 17, 1982	4.8
October 20, 1987	5.3
October 21, 1987	9.1
October 29, 1987	4.9
October 28, 1997	5.1
September 8, 1998	5.1
March 16, 2000	4.8
January 3, 2001	5.0
July 24, 2002	5.7
July 29, 2002	5.4
September 30, 2008	5.4
October 13, 2008	11.6
October 20, 2008	4.8
October 28, 2008	10.8
November 13, 2008	6.9
November 21, 2008	6.3
November 24, 2008	6.5
December 16, 2008	5.1
March 10, 2009	6.4
March 23, 2009	7.1

Figure 8.1 *(Source: Bloomberg)*

all optimism, however. Most stocks fell, especially among the smaller firms, as investors shifted their positions heavily into blue chip stocks in search of safety. Ironically, this was a rally fueled by a large dose of pessimism.

Optimism ran even stronger on October 21, as heavy demand for shares across the board spurred on another 5 percent–plus trading day. To the extent any individual played a role, it was the Fed chairman, Alan Greenspan. Interest rate reductions of course have been a frequent cause of heavy market gains, and it is natural and convenient for reporters to ascribe important central bank actions to their heads. In truth, while leadership matters, rate changes are voted on collectively by the Federal Open Market Committee. In this case, the Fed had been lowering rates and seemed poised to continue in the same direction, and the US dollar had been gaining strength. In short, late October 1987's raging bull was a bounce-back from a market crash, undergirded by some favorable macroeconomic conditions.

October tends to be a volatile month on Wall Street—recall the harrowing Black Monday and Black Thursday of 1929. A decade after the October 1987 rally, a similar one hit the Street. It was similar in that on October 27, 1997, stocks bounced back from a previous pounding for no clear reason other than traders had decided the bloodletting and profit taking of the previous day had been enough. The bears had been so fierce that stock exchanges were forced to shut down early. That was excessive and puzzling, according to Peter Canelo of Morgan Stanley Dean Witter. "Too many stocks have been unfairly trashed," he observed. Encouraged by the sharp reversal, Canelo's firm issued a top-ten equities shopping list.

It became easier to pin record days on the actions of an individual Federal Reserve chairman when that individual was Greenspan. For a unique combination of reasons, the stilted economist attracted obsessive attention among Fed watchers, investors, and even some members of the general public during his chairmanship (1987–2006). As David Sicilia and Jeffrey Cruikshank observed in their study of Greenspan's influence, "our subject has become a mega celebrity—known, respected, feared, scrutinized, consulted, and quoted throughout the world."

In the late summer of 1998, the global financial scene was still reeling from the Russian government's default on its debt. Should the international situation worsen, Greenspan hinted in comments at the September 8, 1998, FOMC meeting, the Fed was prepared to act by lowering rates. As the *Wall Street Journal* recorded the next day, "A few words from Federal Reserve Chairman Alan Greenspan spurred major stock indexes to their biggest point gains in history yesterday." This sharp recovery did not put investors at ease, however, because—like most strong one-day gains—it came on the heels of a long string of losing days or even weeks. In this case, international turmoil had driven down stock markets for seven long weeks, with the final three especially harrowing.

As on October 20, 1987, one-day gains topped 5 percent on March 15, 2000, as investors fled to the safe haven of blue chip stocks. In this case, however, the cause was clear. Beginning slowly in 1995, then accelerating sharply in 1997, investors poured capital into what became known—once it collapsed on that day in 2000 and over the course of the next two years—as the "dot-com bubble." Capital from baby boomer retirement accounts, California venture capitalists, and institutional investors alike had driven up the value of equities to some $3.7 trillion, about $2.6 trillion above the historical trend line. The mania gave us Amazon, Yahoo!, and some other tech pioneers, but the vast majority of "born on the web" and "clicks and bricks" firms failed. On this March day, the *Wall Street Journal* reported, investors "funneled money out of the once-blistering technology sector and into the blue chips." The Nasdaq, trading home to many of the new tech securities, "suffered its third consecutive decline of more than 100 points, leaving it down more than 9% in just three days." Once again, Wall Street's Goliath corporations won as legions of smaller David-like firms faltered. Jon Olesky of Morgan Stanley Dean Witter, perhaps sensing the demise of the dot-com era, remarked, "I would be shocked if this was a one-day event."

During the long and steep slide that indeed followed, the Fed stepped in occasionally, attempting to lessen the carnage. When Greenspan signaled rate moves before doing so, markets typically discounted the future immediately. When he played the game closer to his vest, investors tripped over themselves to read the tea leaves (or the thickness of his briefcase; thicker signaled a likely rate move), and considerable suspense built up around FOMC meetings. Sometimes the Fed even managed to catch Wall Street off guard. The first business day of 2001 (January 2) was just such a day. Early that afternoon, the Fed announced an "unexpected" cut in the federal funds rate of fifty basis points. The Dow immediately shot up 373 points, and closed the day up 299.60 (at 10,945.75).

Markets spiked twice in July 2002. Like many times before, these were rebounds from, as the New York Times put it, "several punishing weeks." The day after the broad market touched a five-year low on July 23, many investors concluded the bottom had been reached. They were also buoyed by announcements from several large companies of plans to buy back their own stock, by short sellers locking in rising prices, and by news of a Congressional agreement on corporate governance and accounting. "Even the arrest of former top executives at Adelphia Communications, who were charged with fraud," the Times reported somewhat dryly, "was a boost." The rally continued for days, feeding on itself, with three broad indexes closing above 5 percent five trading days later, on July 29, 2002.

Looking at the big picture, some investors must have seen the 2002 rally as a bookend to an era of dot-com overexuberance and gargantuan corporate scandals. They were partially correct—Enron, Global Crossing, and ImClone had been brought down by accounting scandals in late 2001, but more such failures were to come. Meanwhile, financial markets began to march upward, driven by a seemingly insatiable hunger for mortgage-backed securities that too often contained unhealthy portions of risky subprime mortgages, which in turn were spun into many varieties of derivatives, some of them arcanely "synthetic."

Some have marked the onset of the collapse as April 2007, when New Century, a real estate investment trust that specialized in subprime mortgages, filed for bankruptcy. But the Dow didn't peak until that October, and the first major milestone in a series of major events did not arrive until March 17, 2008, when the Federal Reserve facilitated the sale of Bear Stearns to JPMorgan Chase by guaranteeing the bad loans on its books. Dominoes fell throughout the year, with September an especially harrowing month, marked by the government takeover of Fannie Mae, Freddie Mac, and AIG; the collapse of Lehman Brothers, Merrill Lynch, and Washington Mutual; and the exit of Goldman Sachs and Morgan Stanley from investment banking. By year end, the Federal funds rate stood at zero, and the Dow was still tracking downward.

Securities markets whipsawed through those fifteen months (January 2008 through March 2009), posting many harrowing declines and bouncing back more than 4 percent on nine different dates, more than 5 percent on five others, and above 10 percent on two. Several of the one-day rallies were sparked by individual or joint actions of public officials, including two key former Wall Street figures: Treasury Secretary Henry "Hank" Paulson Jr. (from Goldman Sachs) and New York Fed Chairman Timothy Geithner (Warburg Pincus). Presidents (George W. Bush and Barack Obama) and Congress also sparked rallies in late 2008 and 2009 by enacting economic stimulus packages.

Chapter 9

Lessons

August 17, 1982, was not only one of the biggest days on Wall Street since the Second World War. It was of course also an exciting day in my career. Even decades later, I remain startled by the effect my shift from bear to bull had on global financial markets, and by the press coverage that followed. The magnitude of those reactions was in some ways even more puzzling because my call came late; as noted in the Introduction, retrospective analysis would show that the secular (long-term) peak in interest rates arrived in October 1981. Still, secular reversals sometimes take months or even years and therefore are often difficult to discern in real time.

Rather, what I am most proud of professionally is what I was able to accomplish at Salomon Brothers in building what became widely recognized as the world's preeminent fixed-income research operation, as well as the fact that I was elevated to serve on the firm's Executive Committee, where I could assert my views. From the early 1960s, when Sidney Homer and I, aided by four assistants, were the firm's fixed-income research department, to the late 1980s, when we employed some 450 researchers

145

in the fixed-income and equity operations, including about fifty with PhDs, Salomon Brothers built a reputation for innovative, comprehensive, rigorous, and independent bond market analysis. Meanwhile, I developed a methodology for forecasting interest rates based on flow of funds analysis, an approach that proved to be accurate enough to attract a large following on the Street.

Economic and financial forecasting is far from an exact science. Unlike predictions in the natural sciences that often rest on the immutable laws of physics and chemistry, business and economics involve human behavior, and therefore carry a large element of uncertainty. In spite of the long-standing view most economists hold, humans are not fully rational actors, always seeking to maximize resources and profits. This view of *homo economicus* fails to account for several biases held by economic actors such as investors, as well as by financial forecasters. I detailed this subject in two of my previous books, so here is a brief summary of a few biases that pose real challenges in the field of economic and business forecasting.

One is herding. That is, most predictions fall within a rather narrow range, deviating little from the prevailing consensus view. After all, there is great comfort in running with the crowd. Those who stand out risk being singled out as very wrong.

Forecasters also tend to rely too heavily on historical data. Much of economics has been built on a methodology that runs something like this. First, historical data about a particular problem—let's use inflation in this example—is collected. With that data, a model is built to predict the rate of inflation for a particular future period. Then the future happens, and the model almost always fails to precisely predict the rate of inflation. The economist then jiggers the model so that it would have predicted the correct outcome, and runs the experiment again. Repeat ad infinitum.

It is not difficult to identify weaknesses in this approach. First, models cannot account for all the variables that might influence the outcome. Also, how does one assign weight or significance to each variable? The economics profession has come to rely heavily on this sort of modeling—the arcane "science" of econometrics, performed by well-paid "quants." It takes a kind of supreme confidence to believe that mathematical equations can predict a future that involves human behavior. And related to these fundamental limitations of economic modeling as applied to the fate of human society (another term for financial forecasting) is an even more fundamental truth: history doesn't repeat itself.

Or, to put it a little differently, history repeats itself, except when it doesn't. Students of financial crises are more sensitive to this problem than many others in economics. Their data show that investor behavior, financial markets, and macroeconomies tend to follow discernible patterns—except during periods of extreme stress, when (depending on one's school of thought) either different rules apply or most of them simply go out the window. The great bond analyst W. Braddock "Brad" Hickman documented this reality in his massive compilations of bond market behavior.

Along with business and economic cycles, structural change over the course of several years or a few decades can play havoc with forecasting. In the early twentieth century, let's recall, the placid Edwardian Era was shattered by world war, which fundamentally reordered economic and financial relations between Europe and the United States. In the 1920s, new financial instruments and institutions fueled an unforeseen binge of credit, household borrowing, and stock market speculation. During the Great Depression, central bank adherence to the international gold standard, a near religion at the time, choked off liquidity and economic recovery. US finance was again restructured during the Second World War, as massive federal borrowing and spending tested Keynesian theories. And so on. Financial models fashioned during any one of these periods would have found themselves quickly outmoded in the next.

As my career at Salomon Brothers unfolded, I was drawn to the larger arena of business and financial markets, in particular the relationship between market behavior and structural changes in financial markets and their implications for monetary policy. That became an enduring theme in my writings, speeches, and interviews. Over the decades, I observed again and again how Federal Reserve officials came up short by failing to fully understand or properly account for the impact of structural changes in financial markets on central bank policy. I recognized early on how the concentration of power in a shrinking number of Wall Street financial firms was, among many other problems, undermining the efficient and competitive operation of markets and amplifying financial instability. It was a troubling trend in the 1980s, and one that I testified about in Congress numerous times. The financial crisis of 2008 only made the problem worse.

Success at forecasting in business and finance will come to those who can focus on spotting structural changes in those fields. Doing so is difficult, to be sure—analogous to standing in the middle of the block and forecasting what will come around the corner. In my case, I was fortunate to recognize early on that the eventual removal of Regulation Q would significantly alter not only the structure of financial markets but also the movement in open market interest rates. That insight was a key component behind my view that interest rates in the 1970s would go much higher than generally expected.

Another common bias that plagues forecasters is that negative news and negative predictions are invariably unwelcome. I can recall no US president, Federal Reserve chair, Council of Economic Advisers head, or US Treasury secretary ever forecasting a business recession.

Humans' biological mechanism for survival is grounded in optimism. Behavioral economists have documented our persistent tendency to underestimate risk and the odds of failure. Negative forecasts are politically unpopular. No one likes to hear bad news—or, in the case of government economic policymakers, wants to be perceived as failing at their jobs. This relates to a more general bias, identified by psychologists, toward optimism in economic decision making: humans tend to underestimate risk and overestimate their likelihood of success.

No one can completely escape these biases, but forecasters should try hard to minimize them. It helps to keep in mind that a forecaster's task is to say what *will* be rather than what *should* be. That means remaining loyal to what the analysis says even if the story it tells is unwelcome, which in turn requires a high level of institutional autonomy. At the same time, forecasters—especially those who rely on elaborate econometric computer models—need to keep in mind the real limitations of their craft. Historical data and conventional patterns can only get forecasters so far.

The episode described in this book begs a couple of forecasting-related questions: Why was I the only private individual since World War II to send the Dow soaring nearly 5 percent in a single day? And is something like that likely to happen again?

Earlier, I emphasized the central role that my long-bearish stance played in drawing enormous attention to and amplifying my change in stance. Simply put, many Wall Streeters reacted strongly to my memo because they concluded, "If Dr. Doom has turned bullish, it must be true." That is only a partial explanation, however, for as described in chapters four and seven, before the summer of 1982, some of my pronouncements already had registered rather sizable impacts—including bearish ones.

Figure 9.1 When William Salomon was the firm's managing partner, he placed a high value on independent research and client relations. (Arthur Brower/The New York Times/REDUX)

These bearish-to-more-bearish episodes cast doubt on a pure bear-to-bull theory, although the length of time I had been bearish surely mattered.

I am of course glad to claim some credit for what happened that eventful day. But that is only part of the story. Another important element was the support my research operations received from Salomon Brothers senior management during the years Billy Salomon was managing director. Other firms at the time either did not protect the independence and integrity of their in-house research as stringently as Salomon Brothers or—more commonly—they simply kept the fruits of their research in house rather than sharing major findings with the wider investment community as we did. As far as I am aware, I was the only research executive to reach the top ranks of a major Wall Street investment house. Rather than toiling away in the trenches, relegated to a support function, I was entrusted with power and responsibility at the highest ranks of the firm so I could not only safeguard the firm's research operations, but also shape its strategic direction.

Along with the challenge of remaining independent but with ample institutional support, forecasters in the future face a much more crowded field than I did when I started at Salomon Brothers. Early in my career I achieved recognition because I was one among a small number of economists who focused on Federal Reserve and US Treasury operations. Today there are legions. That makes the challenge of how to stand out from the crowd even greater. Another lesson: it helps to focus where others do not. My early career analysis in *Prospects for Financial Markets* received much recognition because of its distinctiveness.

Public-sector forecasting is a different matter. In the United States, a handful of public-sector figures will remain capable of roiling markets with economic news—the president and Fed chairman first and foremost, although both are advised to choose their public remarks carefully. More often than not in the public sphere, financial markets are unsettled by news issued through a government agency, such as FOMC interest rate changes, Commerce Department reports on unemployment, or Bureau of Labor Statistics unemployment figures.

What about private-sector figures? Will there be another day when financial markets will respond dramatically to a private-sector forecast? If my case is to serve as a model, a non-government individual capable of significantly moving markets would need a long-established reputation and enough institutional autonomy—protected by holding a role in senior management or, at a minimum, having strong allies there—to express independent views that sometimes might even contradict the interests of his or her firm.

When an economist and his or her firm do not respect each other's boundaries, the quality of the research—and with it the researcher's reputation—are compromised, to the detriment of both sides. Or the relationship dissolves. Earlier, I mentioned that Gary Shilling was recruited by Merrill Lynch as chief economist five years after I joined Salomon Brothers. As Albert Malabre recounts, Shilling soon left Merrill because he tried to be "candid in his forecasts and resent[ed] the repeated muzzling that came from higher-ups at the securities firm." Indeed, as I noted earlier, few welcome bad news or its messenger. Malabre recalls that Shilling's "departure was largely a consequence of a particularly

frank and somewhat pessimistic appraisal of the economic outlook during an interview with me that I subsequently published
in the Dow Jones news wire, which the *Wall Street Journal* oper-
ated and often quoted."

Given current realities on Wall Street, it seems highly unlikely
that we will see this set of conditions for quite some time. Along
with the dramatic rise in financial concentration, the incorporation of Wall Street also threatens research independence. As my
career unfolded, I became increasingly concerned about some of
the consequences (even if unintended) of leading investment firms
going public. I experienced firsthand how the shift from partnership to corporation at Salomon Brothers affected the behavior
of its leaders and major traders. Under the partnership regime,
relationships with clients were valued highly. After incorporation, that relationship became more distant and transactional.
More than that, as a corporation Salomon Brothers came under
increasing pressure to generate short-term profits through greater
risk taking, an approach John Gutfreund was all too eager to
embrace.

Indeed, one of the main reasons I resigned from Salomon
Brothers in April 1988 was that John restructured the firm in
ways that undermined my ability to influence the firm's policies
and strategic direction. Gravely concerned about Salomon Brothers becoming over-leveraged, I had been an outspoken critic of
the firm's move into junk bonds and its departure from the commercial paper and municipal bond businesses. All of this put me
at odds with Gutfreund's regime. When John organized the Office
of the Chairman to replace the Executive Committee, I was left
out of membership—a move he made in part to marginalize my

influence. Sadly, in 1991 Phibro-Salomon was racked by a major Treasury bond trading scandal, and the SEC fined John Gutfreund and forced him to resign. The company staggered along for six more years until it was bought by Travelers Group. By 2003 the Salomon name had disappeared from Wall Street. (For two insightful accounts of the demise of Salomon Brothers, see Mayer, *Nightmare on Wall Street,* and Bookstaber, *A Demon of Our Own Design.*)

The incorporation of Wall Street also worked to undermine the independence of the research function, and therefore of forecasting among many of the leading firms as well. Today's enormous shareholder-owned financial conglomerates have little room for autonomy among their key players, especially those with prominent public profiles.

In so many ways, it all comes back to independence—the independence to research, to analyze, and to speak. Investors can tell whether a forecaster commands these kinds of independence. If he or she does, they listen. If not, they turn away.

Chapter 10

New Realities

Old habits die hard. For all the biases and other limitations that work against accurate forecasting, I would feel uneasy ending this book (my fifth) without a few considerations about American economic, business, and financial life in the near future.

As this book goes to press, economies throughout the world are struggling under the enormous weight of the second global pandemic in a century. In the first half of this chapter, I discuss a series of economic and financial challenges the United States confronted on the eve of COVID-19's rapid spread in this country during the second quarter of 2020. But that section hardly should be considered as strictly "before COVID-19" and no longer relevant to today or to the period after the US is no longer afflicted by the virus. Rather, we should think of the economic and financial damage the virus is inflicting—the topic of the second half of this chapter—as being added to or layered on top of the pre-COVID status quo. And as we will see, COVID-19 is exacerbating existing structural weaknesses, such as the expanding role—and diminishing effectiveness—of Federal Reserve efforts to cope with crisis and ensure economic growth and stability.

Little of what I have to say about either the pre-COVID realities at the start of 2020, or the staggering damage the virus wrought soon thereafter, is uplifting. But at this point in the book, the reader is well familiar with my deep commitment to reporting what I see and conclude, even if it is sobering.

By the beginning of 2020, the US, having emerged from the long tail of the Great Recession a few years earlier, seemed to be humming along. The Dow was setting records, and the unemployment rate had dipped below 4 percent. Was the nation therefore on a sound economic and financial footing? In spite of those positive indicators, it seemed to me that the ever-evolving structure of our financial markets posed new, perhaps even unprecedented, challenges.

Compared with the nation's financial basis in the immediate aftermath of the Second World War, early 2020 was far less secure. In those early postwar decades, financial leverage was exceedingly low and financial institutions were much more constrained by official policy. Equally important was Wall Street's prevailing restrained culture of risk taking. Many participants still held personal, vivid memories of the excesses that led to the collapse of financial markets during the late 1920s and early 1930s.

In contrast to the early postwar decades, financial concentration rose prior to and during the Great Recession and continued to gain momentum in the recovery. Back in 1990, the ten largest financial institutions held about 10 percent of US financial assets. A mere decade later, the figure was at least 80 percent. To be sure, official policymakers have tried to constrain large financial institutions, which are now deemed "too big to fail."

These behemoths are required to take stress tests, and there are procedures in place for their orderly liquidation if they get into serious financial trouble.

At first this seems quite reasonable, but it will eventually lead to even greater financial concentration. When institutions are dissolved, who absorbs the balance sheets? Perhaps, initially, the federal government. Ultimately, however, the assets of failing entities will be absorbed by the remaining giant institutions.

These financial conglomerates have taken on a quasi-monopolistic role. They dominate in market making, investment banking, and money management. From my perspective, they are quasi-public financial utilities—too big to fail when the government rescues the markets from their frailties, yet still able to exercise significant financial entrepreneurship during periods of monetary ease. Meanwhile, during periods of monetary restraint, smaller financial institutions experience disproportionate pressure, and those that collapse typically are absorbed by the too-big-to-fail institutions. The result, again, is greater financial concentration.

For its part, the Federal Reserve has pursued twenty-first-century policies that not only have supported further financial concentration but also have posed significant risks to future financial markets. This is the policy of *monetary moderation*. Its main features are projections for economic growth, inflation, and the likely path of the Federal funds rate. Will the Fed really ever forecast significant change in economic activity such as a recession or jumps in inflation? For reasons I discussed in the previous chapter, I seriously doubt it. Up to now, at least, the central bank's projections have been comforting to financial markets.

In fact, such projections encourage speculation. The Fed's policy of monetary moderation has had a glaringly speculative impact on corporate finance. The yield gap between high- and low-quality corporate bonds continues to be extremely narrow even though the overall quality of corporate debt has deteriorated sharply. The volume of outstanding corporate bonds classified as investment grade has shifted sharply to the low end of this category, while the volume of below-investment-grade bonds has increased sharply.

With the sharp increase in corporate profits in this cycle, isn't it rather surprising that no prominent corporation has come forth to state that it will dedicate a significant portion of its profits to improving its credit rating? Instead, most corporate profits are used to increase dividends or to buy back outstanding shares. Today, only two business corporations enjoy a triple-A rating (Johnson & Johnson and Microsoft). In the 1980s, there were sixty-one. Meanwhile, investment banking departments in the large financial conglomerates are eager to find their clients new candidates for acquisitions or mergers. And the investment banks frequently facilitate such takeovers with loans.

There are many examples of how corporate financing tactics have changed since around the 1980s. Here is just one. Early in my financial career (in the 1950s), the common stock of AT&T was considered an excellent investment for widows and orphans. The $9 cash dividend it paid on its stock was viewed as a firm commitment to the future. In 2018, AT&T bought Time Warner, thereby increasing its total debt to more than $180 billion. The move caused AT&T's credit rating to fall to Baa, just a few steps above junk.

I do not see the financial position of households as substantially improving much in the near future, either, and not only because of the COVID-19 crisis. To be sure, household indebtedness fell in the years immediately after 2008. But it has risen again, and is now above its earlier peaks. The financial footing of households is heavily dependent on rising wages as well as on the absence of flaring interest rates. This is a particular vulnerability for low-income and some middle-income households, where wealth cushions are thin to nonexistent.

Concurrently, the shadow banking system is flourishing. For example, the notional amount of outstanding over-the-counter derivatives contracts totaled $640 trillion in June 2019, and that market has conveniently moved to London and therefore out of the direct oversight of US authorities. The leveraged loan market, where restrictive covenants are light (as they are for most new corporate bond issues), now totals at least $1.4 trillion, up from $700 billion at the end of 2007. The volume of outstanding exchange-traded funds has risen to $5 trillion. And private equity funds are attracting huge inflows of capital, even though these funds are invested on far more liberal terms than in the past.

All of this suggests a conundrum for the financing of future economic growth, even after we emerge from pandemic-related economic shutdowns. Who will be the effective borrowers? The creditworthiness of business corporations may well be stretched, with further borrowing pushing more and more corporations below investment grade. Similarly, greater household borrowing will come at the expense of their credit ratings. Given these constraints, in all likelihood it will be the federal government that fills the GDP financing gap even more than it has in recent years, with the high probability that its credit rating will be lowered a notch or two.

Financial markets depend heavily on the concepts of liquidity and marketability. But these two market dynamics no longer function as they once did. During the early post–World War II period, liquidity was understood to encompass readily convertible assets such as cash on hand, holdings of Treasury bills and commercial paper, and open lines of bank credit. But over time, firms and investors came to define liquidity in terms of a corporation's capacity to borrow. In order to borrow, firms typically issued short-term paper, borrowed short-term from banks, and had back-up lines of credit. A lot of that activity was meant to carry firms through seasonal or cyclical periods of relative capital scarcity. They expected to pay off short-term obligations in a matter of weeks or at most months. But more and more often corporations rolled over these instruments, so that in a fundamental or operational sense they became sources of long-term liquidity. Thus, in today's markets, short-term liabilities are actually long-term liabilities because they are rarely paid off.

As for marketability, it, too, has changed in ways that are not widely understood, even though all market dynamics hinge on it. Even the simplest aspects such as bid and ask prices are part of the lexicon of marketability. Today, there are pricing services for large portfolios, analytics for judging values within and among many of the components that make up our diverse groups of markets, and theories that depend on the validity of marketability. Nevertheless, the concept is flawed, and its weaknesses are becoming more apparent as the structure of the marketplace itself is evolving.

To be sure, the market price of a security hinges on the size of the market, its maturity, its credit quality, and its size. Many adhere to the simplistic view that securities can be sold somewhere close to the price of the last trade. But sale price depends on all the variables I have noted. The size of a security alone will significantly affect marketability. How much trading can actually be done to capture an opportunity suggested by a simple yield spread between two securities, and how much value will it add to a large portfolio?

Here are some other shortcomings to marketability. When assets of lower credit quality come to market, the buyer is never given an estimate of the future magnitude of the trading range under varying market conditions. When there is a high concentration of investments in relatively few institutions, the marketability of such a large pool of securities is reduced. Under these circumstances, who will really participate in the market? Financial concentration worsens this problem by reducing competition among market makers. And increasing concentration in finance and in the nonfinancial sector is bound to lead to more government intervention in the financial intermediation process and a greater role for the Federal Reserve in providing liquidity.

Marketability also plays a central role in the efficient allocation of capital, even though the underpinnings of marketability are somewhat elusive. This is because only a small fraction of outstanding marketable issues is ever traded, while the preponderance of the remaining issues lay dormant but are priced by the relatively small percentage that is traded. Ultimately, the notion that significant assets can be liquidated easily is simply an illusion. In fact, the larger the market participant, the less capable that participant is of liquidating at any kind of predictable price.

It seems clear to me that the combination of deteriorating credit quality, elusive marketability, and high financial concentration has increased the role of the central bank as the lender of last resort, a trend greatly exaggerated by the pandemic. To some extent, market participants may be aware of this reality, and therefore have concluded that downdrafts in financial asset values by, say, 20 or 25 percent will be met by powerful monetary easing. Traditionally, central banks are supposed to play that role when markets get into extreme difficulty—that is, when marketability becomes dysfunctional.

Market participants are aware of this or relearned the lesson from the 2008 debacle. Indeed, given the events of 2008, the general market expectation is that the Federal Reserve will act more quickly and decisively next time, thereby limiting downside market risks. This suggests to me that monetary policy has become a greater captive of financial markets than ever before. Indeed, I would agree with Al Wojnilower's recent comment that "today's Fed also seems to want to be a lender of early resort in order to nip recessions in the bud. However, promoting a public perception that the Fed will always be able to prevent serious recessions and drops in asset prices is a reliable precursor to overspeculations and credit crunches." The fact that the Federal Reserve is becoming captive to the stock market also reinforces my view that such decisive central bank intervention will encourage a continued drop in credit quality. This is because improvements in the quality of outstanding debt depend on reductions in outstanding weaker debt.

Alas, reducing the proportion of weak debt is a very difficult goal to achieve in a developed society. During flush times, as growing firms and industries call for even greater credit, lenders are happy to feed their appetites. The harsh reality is that weaker borrowers typically are weeded out by sustained economic slumps or crushed by competitors (that is, in the words of Austrian economist Joseph Schumpeter, by "the gales of creative destruction"). In other words, low-quality debt tends to get flushed out not through premeditated, gradualist, managerial decision making, but by capitalism's roughest edges—widespread business failures and bankruptcy.

Government intervention also may be spurred on by the continuing advance of technology—especially the Information Revolution—not only in finance but in the larger economy. The Industrial Revolution of the eighteenth century had an even greater impact than the Information Revolution, at least up to now. However, the Industrial Revolution eventually led to an increase in the power of labor. After decades (or centuries, depending on the country) of exploitation, workers banded together to form industry-wide labor unions, and collective bargaining helped drive wages higher, becoming a restraint on corporate profits.

At least so far, today's workers have not devised effective ways to counter the downward pressure on wages exerted by the worldwide Information Revolution and the globalization of labor markets. The power of unions has declined, while corporations, aided by vast improvements in methods of production, have taken advantage of lower labor costs everywhere. More than that, corporate mergers and consolidations have led to great market concentration in many sectors (not just finance), which in turn has given businesses greater influence over the pricing structure for their products and services. These trends are clearly reflected in the overall rise in corporate profits (including those in the financial sector) as a percentage of GDP, as compared with a rather modest recent rise in wages. I suspect this divergence will be difficult to reverse. Vast improvements in technology and the delivery of information seem far from over.

Information is indeed power. August 17, 1982, illustrates the point. The way economic and investment information reaches Wall Street has already changed considerably over the last forty years, which may be yet another reason why no private-sector individual since has caused the markets to roar (or collapse) to the same degree. It is interesting to note that no formidable financial forecaster has emerged on social media.

The United States remains the world's coronavirus hotspot as of this writing, and there is great uncertainty about the extent of damage or virus control in many parts of the Global South and Eastern Europe. In the financial sector, markets and official policies are and will continue to be deeply affected for years to come. Here is a brief summary of likely outcomes in the United States.

Business corporations will continue to suffer declines in sales and profits until most of the population becomes immune (through vaccination or infection). In an effort to cope, they will shrink or eliminate dividends and bring to an end long-standing stock repurchase programs. Most importantly, the credit quality of corporate debt will deteriorate even further, accelerating a troubling trend already underway during the recent economic expansion. Whether the credit rating agencies will react to this development with alacrity is questionable. Yet that may not really matter because markets quite often lower the price they are willing to pay for corporate debt when its quality weakens.

In the household sector, consumption will continue only at a moderate pace in response to high unemployment in spite of strong fiscal policy actions designed to bolster household consumption. In contrast, new housing activity should do reasonably well, as many heads of households rethink their preference for urban living and relocate to suburbs.

In the government arena, the pandemic is bringing to the fore three striking developments. First, state and local governments are coming under extreme financial pressure. Along with sharp increases in their expenditures for virus-related emergency measures, they will continue to see steep declines in revenues from sales, real estate, and income taxes. Their dependence on the federal government is increasing. That reality has both financial and political implications because many state and local governments could see their political independence eroded by their weakening financial status.

Second, the coronavirus has motivated the US federal government to dramatically increase its outlays in an effort to offset some of the precipitous shortfall in private-sector spending. This is a laudable policy. But turning down the federal spending spigot will involve difficult political decisions. Who will endure the first cutbacks? Such choices may not necessarily be decided on economic grounds. In the meantime, federal government deficits of $2 trillion to $3 trillion are very likely, and the US government's credit rating probably will be lowered, although I doubt that would have much market significance.

The most striking impact of the coronavirus may well be centered on monetary policy. Before the virus became a significant factor in the United States, interest rates generally were at record lows. Once the economy began to collapse, the Federal Reserve cut rates twice, and may take them even lower, although little room to maneuver remains. At the same time, working through a special purpose vehicle, the central bank has agreed to buy private-sector debt—obligations of households, municipalities, and corporations. The Fed also will continue to buy US government securities outright when it deems that necessary to stabilize and strengthen the markets. Its holdings of these securities now total over $5 trillion (after reaching a post–Great Recession low of $3.6 trillion in September 2019).

All these measures, some breaking with historical precedent, will accelerate the troubling trend already underway toward reducing the central bank's quasi-independence. It is rapidly becoming more of a direct arm of the federal government. I still recall from nearly seven decades ago when, through the Fed–Treasury Accord of March 1951, the central bank won a hard-fought battle for much greater independence after being compelled to help monetize the national debt during and immediately following the Second World War. Now another international emergency threatens to return the Federal Reserve to that kind of more subservient role from which it may find itself very hard to extricate.

The strong forces at work in pre-COVID and COVID America that I have just reviewed—especially financial concentration and the Federal Reserve's waning independence—are undermining the nature of our political economy. They are joined by other very troubling recent developments. Free trade is being dismantled as treaties are being abrogated. The free movement of labor is constrained by walls and edicts. Competition enforcement in business and finance is lagging and tardy. The anti-monopoly trustbusting that thrived under President Theodore Roosevelt is long gone. Many businesses now enjoy a global reach, allowing them to post noncompetitive prices. And I've just outlined a number of ways in which financial markets are undermining competition.

Taken together, these trends pose a serious threat to the very nature of our political economy. It is not too much to say that American capitalism itself is under siege.

Adam Smith remains a useful guide to the hallmarks of capitalism. In *The Wealth of Nations* (1776), he argued that humans innately strive for material progress, and the best way to get there is through unfettered competition, the division of labor, and free trade. Smith argued that the state should play a limited role in economic affairs. Governments should be properly confined to national security, the rule of law—including the protection of private property—and the provision of a few public goods such as education. He also cautioned against sharp class divisions that might idle rich people and exploit workers. "No society can surely be flourishing and happy, of which the far greater part of the members are poor and miserable," he warned. Smith hoped that whole societies could be enriched through the striving of individual members.

Capitalism in America is rapidly being replaced by statism—a form of political economy in which the state exercises substantial centralized control over social and economic affairs. In the US, the federal government and the Federal Reserve sit atop our particular form of statism. The federal government has a vast capacity to tax, borrow, and reallocate funds. Federal debt owed to the public now exceeds $20 trillion, and much more can be borrowed. For some time to come, the US dollar will remain the

Figure 10.1 Adam Smith, the great eighteenth-century Scottish philosopher and economist, understood the virtues of competition. *(Sueddeutsche Zeitung Photo/Alamy Stock Photo)*

key reserve currency, and overseas investors continue to prefer US government bonds over most other securities.

In contrast, the creditworthiness of state and local governments has come under acute pressure because of the coronavirus pandemic, forcing many of them to seek federal help. For some time to come, states and localities will be financially beholden to the federal government, weakening their independence while strengthening the central authority. That is not the kind of shared and distributed power the founders envisioned for our system of federalism.

The erosion of the Federal Reserve's quasi-independence is contributing to the emerging statism. In previous crises the Fed was helpfully supportive. During the Second World War, it stabilized yields on government securities. In the 2008 financial crisis, it bailed out prominent financial institutions, engaged in quantitative easing, forced large banks to accept government capital, and lowered interest rates sharply. But the Fed's response to the pandemic has been far more open-ended. It is buying not only federal, state, and municipal bonds but also corporate bonds—including low-quality issues, mortgage obligations, and exchange-traded bond funds. The central bank is also working with the Treasury to get loans to small and medium-sized businesses. Astonishingly, the Fed's balance sheet has swelled from about $3.8 trillion in August 2019 to some $7.4 trillion at the end of 2020. And financial markets have come to expect the Fed to intervene in response to any sharp decline in equity prices.

Before the pandemic, the Fed had made considerable progress in reducing the size of its balance sheet. But now we can expect an even more significant increase in the magnitude of its intervention. With President-Elect Joseph R. Biden's late 2020 announcement that he would appoint former Federal Reserve Chair Janet Yellen to his cabinet as Treasury Secretary, the linkage between the Fed and the US government has been tightened even more. In the very near term, as the new economic recovery takes hold, there will likely be no difference in economic policy views between Yellen and Fed Chairman Jerome Power. But if differences emerge by late 2021, they may call into question Mr. Powell's reappointment to a second term at the head of the central bank.

With the federal government and the Fed firmly joined at the hip, the transformation of capitalism into statism is gaining momentum, perhaps irreversibly. Not only is this a great departure from the vision of America's founders, I suspect it is also not the kind of economic system most Americans living today want to leave for future generations.

BIBLIOGRAPHY

Aliber, Robert Z., and Charles P. Kindleberger. 2017. *Manias, Panics, and Crashes.* 7th ed. New York: Palgrave Macmillan.

Bailyn, Bernard. 1994. *Bernard Bailyn on the Teaching and Writing of History: Responses to a Series of Questions.* Hanover, NH: University Press of New England.

Bloomberg, Michael, with Matthew Winkler. (1997) 2001. *Bloomberg by Bloomberg.* New York: Wiley.

Bogen, Jules I., Major B. Foster, Marcus Nadler, and Raymond Rodgers. 1947. *Money and Banking.* 3rd ed. New York: Prentice-Hall.

Bookstaber, Richard. 2007. *A Demon of Our Own Design: Markets, Hedge Funds, and the Perils of Financial Innovation.* Hoboken, NJ: Wiley.

Chancellor, Edward. 1999. *Devil Take the Hindmost: A History of Financial Speculation.* New York: Farrar, Straus and Giroux.

Eichengreen, Barry. 1996. *Golden Fetters: The Gold Standard and the Great Depression, 1919–1939.* Oxford: Oxford University Press.

Geisst, Charles R. 2018. *Wall Street: A History.* 4th ed. New York: Oxford University Press.

Hayek, F. A. (1944) 1994. *The Road to Serfdom.* Chicago: University of Chicago Press.

Heller, Walter W., and Milton Friedman. 1969. *Monetary Policy vs. Fiscal Policy.* New York: W.W. Norton.

Hickman, W. Braddock. 1958. *Corporate Bond Quality Investor Experience.* Princeton, NJ: Princeton University Press.

Homer, Sidney. 1975. "The Historical Evolution of Today's Bond Market." In *Explorations in Economic Research* 2, no. 3 (*Regional Stock Exchanges in the Central Market System*), 378–389. Cambridge, MA: National Bureau of Economic Research.

Homer, Sidney, and Richard Sylla. 2005. *A History of Interest Rates.* 4th ed. Hoboken, NJ: Wiley.

Iversen, Torben, and David Soskice. 2019. *Democracy and Prosperity: Reinventing Capitalism Through a Turbulent Century.* Princeton, NJ: Princeton University Press.

Kaufman, Henry. 1975. "Needed: A Breakthrough in Economic Thought." Salomon Brothers essay, September 2.

Kaufman, Henry. 1979. "The Increasing Risks When the Economy Slips from Its Moorings." Salomon Brothers essay, March 19.

Kaufman, Henry. 2000. *On Money and Markets: A Wall Street Memoir.* New York: McGraw Hill.

Kaufman, Henry. 2009. *The Road to Financial Reformation: Warnings, Consequences, Reforms.* Hoboken, NJ: Wiley.

Kaufman, Henry. 2016. *Tectonic Shifts in Financial Markets: People, Policies, and Institutions.* New York: Palgrave Macmillan.

Lewis, Michael. 1989. *Liar's Poker: Rising Through the Wreckage on Wall Street.* New York: W.W. Norton.

Lowenstein, Roger. 2004. *Origins of the Crash: The Great Bubble and Its Undoing.* New York: Penguin.

Lowenstein, Steven M. 1989. *Frankfurt on the Hudson: The German-Jewish Community of Washington Heights, 1933–1983, Its Structure and Culture.* Detroit, MI: Wayne State University Press.

Mackay, Charles. (1841) 2006. *Extraordinary Popular Delusions and the Madness of Crowds.* Petersfield, UK: Harriman House.

Madden, John T., and Marcus Nadler. 1929. *Foreign Securities: Public and Mortgage Bank Bonds—An Analysis of the Financial, Legal and Political Factors.* New York: Ronald Press.

Madden, John T., Marcus Nadler, and Harry C. Sauvain. 1937. *America's Experience as a Creditor Nation.* New York: Prentice-Hall.

Malabre, Albert L., Jr. 1994. *Lost Prophets: An Insider's History of the Modern Economists.* Boston: Harvard Business School Press.

Mayer, Martin. 1993. *Nightmare on Wall Street: Salomon Brothers and the Corruption of Wall Street.* New York: Simon & Schuster.

Nadler, Marcus. 1933. "The Partial Abandonment of the Gold Standard, 1931–1932." *Annuals of the Academy of Political and Social Sciences* 165 (January): 202–206.

Nadler, Paul S. 2001. "Memories of My Father—Marcus Nadler." *The Secured Lender* 57 (November–December): 134.

Pope, Alexander. (1711) 2013. *An Essay on Criticism.* Cambridge, UK: Cambridge University Press.

Reinhart, Carmen M., and Kenneth S. Rogoff. 2009. *This Time Is Different: Eight Centuries of Financial Folly.* Princeton, NJ: Princeton University Press.

Salomon, William. 1981. Letter to the members of the Salomon Brothers Executive Committee, August 10. Personal copy in possession of the author.

Schmeelk, Richard J. 2007. *Mr. Canada: Adventures of an Investment Banker Inside and Outside Business.* New York: Twin Dolphin Books.

Sicilia, David B., and Jeffrey L. Cruikshank. 2000. *The Greenspan Effect: Words That Move the World's Markets.* New York: McGraw Hill.

Silber, William L. 2012. *Volcker: The Triumph of Persistence.* New York: Bloomsbury Press.

Sobel, Robert. 1986. *Salomon Brothers, 1910–1985: Advancing to Leadership.* New York: Salomon Brothers.

Sobel, Robert. 1991. *The Life and Times of Dillon Read.* New York: Truman Talley Books.

Straumann, Tobias. 2019. *1931: Debt, Crisis, and the Rise of Hitler.* Oxford: Oxford University Press.

Temin, Peter. *Lessons from the Great Depression.* 1991. Cambridge, MA: MIT Press.

Thomas, Michael M. 1982. *Someone Else's Money.* New York: Simon & Schuster.

Tooze, Adam. 2018. *Crashed: How a Decade of Financial Crises Changed the World.* New York: Viking.

Volcker, Paul A., and Christine Harper. 2018. *Keeping at It: The Quest for Sound Money and Good Government.* New York: PublicAffairs.

Warburton, Peter. 2000. *Debt and Delusion: Central Bank Follies That Threaten Economic Disaster.* London: Penguin Books.

Wojnilower, Albert M. 1980. "The Central Role of Credit Crunches in Recent Financial History." *Brookings Papers on Economic Activity* 2: 277–339.

Wojnilower, Albert M. 2002. Interview of Albert M. Wojnilower
    conducted by Robert L. Hetzel, August 29, Federal Reserve Bank
    of Boston.
Wolf, Martin. 2014. *The Shifts and the Shocks: What We've
    Learned—And Have Still to Learn—from the Financial Crisis.*
    New York: Penguin.
Wolfe, Tom. 1987. *The Bonfire of the Vanities.* New York: Picador.

NOTES

CHAPTER 1 – THE DAY

Page 12: **I soon discovered…** The August 17, 1982 news stories recounted in the beginning of this chapter were reported in the *New York Times* and *Wall Street Journal* editions for that day.

Page 13: **Wriston and I disagreed…** See chapter 7 of my previous book, *Tectonic Shifts in Financial Markets*.

Page 28: **"Most of the men…"** Lewis, p. 63.

CHAPTER 3 – INTELLECTUAL ROOTS

Page 62: **Marcus Nadler was born…** Paul S. Nadler.

Page 64: **A few years after he was hired…** Bogen.

Page 65: **"Experience during major panics…"** Bogen, p. 242.

Page 65: **"the reality of a financial…"** Kaufman (2016), p. 165.

Page 66: **"The various kinds of collectivism…"** Hayek, p. 63.

Page 66: **In an important new book…** Iversen and Soskice, p. vii.

Page 67: **The two positions…** Heller and Friedman, which includes published versions of the two talks as well as edited versions of the exchanges that followed their formal remarks.

Page 68: **"an even match"** Erich Heinemann, "Friedman-Heller Debate Proves an Even Match," *New York Times*, Nov. 15, 1968.

CHAPTER 4 – WHY I WAS BEARISH FOR SO LONG

Page 72: **According to business writer Martin Mayer...** Mayer, p. 80.

Page 73: **Elsewhere I have written...** Kaufman (2000), pp. 37–39.

Page 73: **In his lively history...** Malabre, pp. 51–52.

Page 74: **"When I first encountered these two men..."** Malabre, p. 52.

Page 75: **As business writer Martin Mayer noted...** Mayer, p. 81.

Page 78: **"three or four times a week,"** Mayer, p. 81.

Page 80: **In a Sunday *New York Times* essay...** Henry Kaufman, "Inflation (Not Oil) as the Real Culprit," *New York Times*, Jan. 27, 1974.

Page 80: **Late that summer...** "Meet the New Jeremiahs," *Newsweek*, July 29, 1972.

Page 81: **In a 1975 talk...** Kaufman (1975).

Page 82: **For the first eight years...** Kaufman (2016), p. 21.

Page 82: **This long and dismal record...** Kaufman (1979).

Page 84: **The late esteemed Harvard historian...** Bailyn, p. 35.

Page 86: **To be yourself...** Pope.

Page 88: **"So there I was..."** Bloomberg, p. 1.

Page 90: **"I handed to you..."** Salomon letter in possession of the author.

CHAPTER 5 – ALBERT M. WOJNILOWER, "DR. DEATH"

Page 93: A May 1981 *Time* magazine... Charles Alexander, "Those Bad News Bears," *Time,* May 25, 1981.

Page 94: He was born in Vienna... Biographical sources for Mr. Wojnilower include Wojnilower (2002); www.gailfosler.com/albert-m-wojnilower (accessed Aug. 9, 2018); and Wojnilower correspondence with the author.

Page 95: During those years (1970–1977)... Henry Scott-Stokes, "Reactions Very for Economists on Fed Change," *New York Times,* Dec. 30, 1977.

Page 97: By the time Wojnilower... Sobel (1991), pp. 202–204, 244.

Page 99: "Wall Street's two most influential..." Vartanig G. Vartan, "Market Place: Still No Letup in Bull Market," *New York Times,* May 31, 1983.

Page 100: That rigor was on full display... Wojnilower (1980).

Page 100: "The key observation..." Wojnilower (1980), p. 277.

Page 100: The implications of this finding... Wojnilower (1980), p. 232.

Page 101: In late 1983... Dec. 4, 1983.

Page 104: The next day... Vartanig G. Vartan, "Short-Term Rates Drop; Prime Rate is Reduced," *New York Times,* Aug. 17, 1982; and Tom Herman and Jill Bettner, "Treasury Bill Rates Plummet to 2-Year Low," *Wall Street Journal,* Aug. 17, 1982.

CHAPTER 6 – CRITICS, THREATS, AND HUMOR

Page 111: As *American Banker* accurately reported... *American Banker*, "How Lovely to Be Famous," Dec. 1, 1982.

Page 111: In his signature self-deprecating style... Russell Baker, "Ben Bolt is in the Street," *New York Times*, Aug. 25, 1982; reprinted as "Poor Henry Kaufman," *Institutional Investor*, Nov. 1982, p. 16.

Page 111: Here are a few passages... Eric Nicol, "A Life in the Day of Henry Kaufman," *The Province Sun*, Sept. 5, 1982.

Page 113: Sidney Rutberg of the *Daily News Record*... Sidney Rutberg, "Stocks Soar on Lousy Biz, He Tells the Kid" *Daily News Record*, Aug. 23, 1982.

Page 114: The Street's mind pictured... Thomas, pp. 469–470.

CHAPTER 7 – GROWING PRESSURES

Page 122: As the *Wall Street Journal* reported... Tom Herman and Edward P. Foldessy, "Bond Prices Plunge on Unexpected Surge Of $1.4 Billion in Basic U.S. Money Supply, *Wall Street Journal*, Jan. 5, 1982.

Page 122: When we shared... Vartanig G. Vartan, "Dow Slides 17.22; Ends At 865.30, *New York Times*, Jan. 6, 1982.

Page 122: Several observers pointed out... Articles in the papers cited all appeared Jan. 5 or 6, 1982, except the *ABA Banking Journal*, which referred to my twenty-year debt warning in its Jan. 1982 edition.

Page 122: In the nation's heartland... "Henry Kaufman," *The Evansville Press*, Jan. 4, 1982.

Page 123: As a writer for the influential... Sally Heineman, "Credit Mart Atmosphere In Disarray," *The Journal of Commerce*, Jan. 11, 1982.

Page 124: The *Chicago Tribune* observed... Bill Neikirk, "Economy in 1982 at crossroads, for better or worse, *Chicago Tribune*, Jan. 8, 1982.

Page 124: As Karen W. Arenson... Karen W. Arenson, "The Kaufman Mystique Grows: When Salomon Brothers' Economist Sneezes Traders on Wall Street Stand to Catch a Cold," *International Herald Tribune*, Jan. 17, 1982.

Page 124: *Forbes* dubbed me... "A Sober Year," *Forbes*, Jan. 4, 1982.

Page 124: London's *Economist* coined "Kaufmania" "Will Wall Street Catch Kaufmania?" *The Economist*, Jan. 9, 1982.

Page 124: The *Chicago Tribune* claimed... Bill Neikirk, "Economy in 1982 at crossroads, for better or worse, *Chicago Tribune*, Jan. 8, 1982.

Page 124: In a major essay for *Barron's*... Jan. 11, 1982.

Page 124: Similarly, *Forbes* concluded... "A Sober Year," *Forbes*, Jan. 4, 1982.

Page 125: Striking a more tongue-in-cheek tone... "No Springtime for Henry," *Journal of Commerce*, March 18, 1982.

Page 125: Reacting to my 1982 forecasts... Jerome Cahill, "Weidenbaum: surge due in mid-'82," *Daily News*, Jan. 13, 1982.

Page 125: Revealingly, Weidenbaum was evasive... Bailey
Morris, "Reagan policies spell tragedy, says Kaufman,
Financial Australian, March 19, 1982.

Page 125: For his part, US Treasury Secretary... Peter Brimelow,
"Credit and Creditability: Henry Kaufman v. Supply-Side
Economics," *Barron's*, Jan. 11, 1982.

Page 125: But by July... Jerome Cahill, "Recovery coming in
like a lamb, *Daily News*, July 19, 1982.

Page 126: Already losing influence... "Henry Kaufman," *The
Evansville Press*, Jan. 4, 1982.

Page 126: Not satisfied with labeling me... Maxwell Newton,
"Gang of 6 ambushing Reagan, *New York Post*, March 31,
1982.

Page 126: A couple of months after that... Maxwell Newton,
"Tax-cut foes get panicky," *New York Post*, May 18, 1982.

Page 127: Following the bear market... Maxwell Newton,
"Kaufman's Views Face Big Test in '82," *New York Post*, Jan.
9, 1982.

Page 127: When bond traders met in Boston in May "Portfolio
Managers to Henry K.: 'You're Wrong,'" *Bondweek*, May 17,
1982.

Page 127: The same month as the *Bondweek* article... "The
Great AIBD Heist," *Euromoney*, May 1982.

Page 128: As I explained to a writer... Marilyn Wilson,
"Monetarism Under Fire," *Dun's Business Month*, May 1982

Page 128: In March I had been widely quoted... See, for
example, John D. Baxterm "Financial Squeeze Makes
Companies Cry 'Uncle.'" *Iron Age*, April 23, 1982.

Page 128: Three months later... Henry Kaufman, "Danger: Too Much Turbulence," *Challenge*, May–June 1982.

Page 128: Hardly, as I explained... "Where Interest Rates Go From Here [Henry Kaufman interview]," *U.S. News & World Report*, April 12, 1982.

Page 129: As Wade McGowan... John G. Powers, "Henry Kaufman: Market Mover Sounds a Warning," *Commodities* magazine, July 1982.

Page 129: The point was driven home... "A Bear Called Henry Makes Wall Street Chicken Out," *The Economist*, July 17, 1982.

Page 129: Later that month (July 23)... "Stocks step along, then fade in finish," *Daily News*, July 23, 1982.

CHAPTER 8 – OTHER RECORD
DAYS ON WALL STREET

Page 138: The first instance (May 26, 1970)... John J. Abele, "Dow Up By 32.04," *New York Times*, May 28, 1970.

Page 138: "Yesterday was the first..." Beatrice E. Garcia, "Market Lifted by Blue-Chip Rally as Volatility Hits Smaller Issues," *Wall Street Journal*, Oct. 21, 1987.

Page 139: Optimism ran even stronger... Victor J. Hillery, "Late Surge Sends Industrials Up 2.86 to 1036.98 on Volume of 122 Million," *Wall Street Journal*, Oct. 22, 1982.

Page 140: It was similar... Sam Webb, et al., "Global Plunge Softened by U.S. Rebound," *Wall Street Journal*, Oct. 29, 1997; and Gregory Zuckerman, "Treasurys Tumble in

184   **NOTES**

Second-Biggest Fall of Year As Investor Dump Bonds to Catch
Rise in Stocks," *Wall Street Journal*, Oct. 29, 1997.

Page 140: "Too many stocks..." Suzanne McGee, "Stocks Burst
Back by 337.17 Points on Record Volume as Bonds Drop,"
Wall Street Journal, Oct. 29, 1997.

Page 140: "our subject has become..." Sicilia and Cruikshank,
p. *x*.

Page 141: "a few words..." E. S. Browning, "Dow Industrials
Jump 380.53 to 8020," *Wall Street Journal*, Sept. 9, 1998.

Page 141: On this March day... E. S. Browning, "Blue Chips
Surge 320.17 as Nasdaq Skids Again," *Wall Street Journal*,
March 16, 2000.

Page 142: The first business day of 2001... Karen Talley, "Rate
Cut by Fed Fuels Stocks; IBM and American Express Jump,"
Wall Street Journal, Jan. 4, 2001.

Page 142: Like many times before... Jonathan Fuerbringer,
"Battered for Weeks, Dow Enjoys Its Biggest Daily Gain Since
'87," *New York Times*, July 25, 2002.

Page 143: The rally continued for days... Jonathan Fuerbringer,
"Broad Rally Sends Stock Up 5 Percent," *New York Times*,
July 30, 2002.

CHAPTER 9 - LESSONS

Page 147: The great bond analyst... Hickman.

Page 152: As Albert Malabre recounts... Malabre, p. 52.

CHAPTER 10 - NEW REALITIES

Page 162: Indeed, I would agree... Memorandum by Albert
Wojnilower, "Growing Steadily, Dec. 13, 2019, in the author's
possession.

INDEX

A

ABC, 45
accounting scandals, 143
Adams, Mel, 36–43
Adams & Rinehart, Inc., 29, 35–45
Adelphia Communications, 142
AIG, 143
Amazon, 141
American Banker, 111
American Bankers Association, 122
American Economic Association, 124
American National Bank & Trust, 18
Anadarko Production Co., 31
Arendt, Hannah, 66
Arenson, Karen W., 124
Argentina, currency of, 134
Armco Steel, 87
asset marketability, 65
Associated Press, 36
ATMs, 4
AT&T, 158
Aubrey G. Lanston & Co., 97
August 17, 1982, 1–8, 11–29
    author's prediction of interest rates
        on, 1, 8, 18–21, 24, 33–34
    bond market on, 31
    and earlier bull markets, 138, 139
    historical context for, 1–5
    interest rate changes on, 29
    and interest rate secular cycle, 5–8

Salomon Brothers Executive
    Committee meeting on, 11, 17–25
trading on, 28–29
and Wojnilower's interest rate
    forecast, 104
Avco Financial Services, Inc., 31

B

"bad news bears," 93
Bailyn, Bernard, 84
Baker, Russell, 111, 112
Banco Ambrosiano, 134
Bankers Trust, 16, 29
bank failures, 133, 134
banking
    commercial, 65, 97
    investment (*see* investment banking)
    New Deal legislation on, 97
    regulation and deregulation in,
        102–103
    shadow banking system, 159
Banking Journal, 122
banks
    first appearance of, 3
    prime rates of, 16, 29
Barron's, 36, 124
BBC, 45
bearish views of author, 71–91
    and attitude toward inflation, 82
    and business cycle's relation to
        interest rates, 80

central role of, 150, 151
change in, 81, 145, 150, 151
and commitment to research, 71–72
and excessive debt creation, 82–83
and "Fed watching," 72, 73
and historical events, 84–85
Homer's influence on, 73
and late 1970s interest rate forecasts,
    83–84
in late 1981 and early 1982, 121 (see
    also pressures concerning forecasts)
and Phibro-Salomon merger, 87–90
and research publications, 74–78
and Salomon research operation,
    78–79
and structural changes on Wall Street,
    83
unpopularity of, 127–129
and US economy in 1970s, 79–82
Bear Stearns, 143
Beckner, Steve, 44
Begin, Menachem, 12
behavioral economy, 149
below-investment-grade corporate bonds,
    158
"Ben Bolt is in the Street" (Baker), 111,
    112
Bennett, Bob, 36
Beretz, Hal, 23, 86–87
Bernhard, Robert, 88
Bianco,Salvador Jorge, 13
biases in forecasting, 146–149
Biden, Joseph R., 170
"big data" age, 7
Bloomberg, Michael, 88–89
Blue Chip Report, 77
"The Bogus Issue of the Deficit"
    (Wojnilower), 101
bond market(s). see also financial markets
    after modified stance on interest
        rates, 123
    on August 17, 1982, 1, 31

author's influence on movements of,
    129
author's position on, 81, 134
early August rally in, 130–131
effect of interest rate prediction on,
    24–25
in July and August, Bond Market
    Roundup on, 130, 131
Salomon Brothers' analyses of, 146
and Salomon Brothers fixed-income
    research, 71
size of, 5
yield upswing in, 132–133
Bond Market Review, 74
Bond Market Roundup, 74, 130, 131
bond prices, 3
"Bond Prices Soar and Rates Plunge In
    One of Biggest Rallies on Record" (Wall
    Street Journal), 47
bonds. see also US government bonds
    author's position on, 80, 81
    corporate, 158
    Fed's buying of, 169
    interest rates on, 134
    long-term, interest rates on, 5–7
Bondweek, 127
The Bonfire of the Vanities (Wolfe), 26–27
Bookstaber, Richard, 143
branch banking, 4
Brimelow, Peter, 124
Brinkley, David, 45
Brookings Institution, 100
budget deficit(s), 14–15. see also national
    debt
    in early 1980s, 101–102
    impact of COVID-19 crisis on,
        165–166
    and Reaganomics, 123–124
bullish position of author
    on bonds, 81
    on interest rates, 129
    shift from bearish stance to, 145,
        150, 151

bull markets (1945–2019), 138–144
  and 2002 rally, 143
  April 2007 onset of collapse, 143
  Greenspan's influence on, 140–141
  January 2, 2001, 139, 142
  from January 2008 through March
    2009, 139, 143–144
  July, 2002, 139, 142–143
  March 15, 2000, 139, 141–142
  May 27, 1970, 138, 139
  October, 1987, 138–140
  October 27, 1997, 139, 140
  September 8, 1998, 139, 141
Burns, Arthur F., 82, 95
Bush, George W., 144
business cycle, interest rates and, 80, 81
businesses
  impact of COVID-19 crisis on, 164
  and market concentration, 164
  stock prices and interest rates
    monitored by, 2
business forecasting field. see economic
  and business forecasting
business investments
  in 1970s, 82
  and federal appetite for credit,
    101–102
  total versus net, 101
Business Today, 36

C

Canelo, Peter, 140
The Cape Codder, 116
capital allocation, marketability and,
  161–162
capitalism, 66–67n, 67, 167, 170
capital markets, 75
Carrington, Tim, 36
CBS Morning News, 45
central banks, role of, 162. see also
  Federal Reserve

"The Central Role of Credit Crunches
  in Recent Financial History"
  (Wojnilower), 100
Chicago Board of Trade, 29
Chicago Tribune, 124
"A Chronology: How The Stock Market
  Scored Record Rise," 30
Citibank, 13–14, 29, 95, 96
class divisions, Smith on, 167
Cohen, Laurie, 44
collectivism, 66, 67
Columbia University, 61, 62, 94, 95
Comments on Credit, 75
commercial banking, 65, 97
Commodities Magazine, 36
commodities trading, securities trading
  versus, 87–88
Commodity News, 36
communism, 66
Congress, one-day rally sparked by, 144
consumer spending
  in 1970s, 82
  in 1980s, 133
  impact of COVID-19 crisis on, 165
Continental Illinois National Bank and
  Trust Co. of Chicago, 102
corporate bonds, 158
corporate borrowing
  in 1970s, 80
  and federal appetite for credit, 101
  and liquidity, 160
corporations
  financing tactics of, 158
  impact of COVID-19 crisis on,
    164–165
  profits of, 164
Courier Express, 52
COVID-19 (coronavirus) pandemic, 138
  and financial position of households,
    159
  impact of, 164
  likely outcomes for the United States,
    164–166

and political economy, 167–170
status quo preceding, 155–164 (*see also* new realities)
"Credit and Creditability" (Brimelow), 124
credit availability
    in 1920s, 147–148
    in 1970s, 83
    credit crunches, 100–101
    and interest rates, 2–3
credit crunches, 100–101
credit demands
    in 1970s, 80
    creating flow model for, 76–78
    research on, 75, 76
    Wojnilower on, 100–101
credit quality
    in 1970s, 83
    deterioration of, 65
    impact of COVID-19 crisis on, 164–165
    and marketability, 161
    Wojnilower's dissertation on, 95
Credit Suisse, 97n
criticisms of author's forecasts, 108, 121
Cruikshank, Jeffrey, 140–141
"curbstone brokers," 3
currencies, 67, 134
cyclical trends, 132, 133

D

Daily News, 36, 129
Daily News Record, 113–114
Daily Telegraph (London), 44
death threats, 108
debt creation, in 1970s, 82–83
debt crisis, in Latin America, 13
debt structure, economic recovery and, 81
deficit spending, Keynesian view of, 68. *see also* budget deficit(s)
democracy, capitalism and, 66–67n, 67
Democracy and Prosperity (Iversen and Soskice), 66–67n

A Demon of Our Own Design (Bookstaber), 143
depressions, 4, 128–129, 148
deregulation
    in 1970s, 82–83
    in 1980s, 102
derivatives, 143, 159
Dillon Read, 97
Dominican Republic, 13
dot-com boom and bust (1995–2002), 138, 141–143
Dow Jones, interview request from, 36
Dow Jones Industrial Average, 29, 51, 55
    and author's bullish position on bonds, 81
    in early 2020, 156
    at end of 2008, 143
    on January 2, 2001, 142
    October 2007 peak in, 143
    record days for, 138, 139
"Dow Soared by 38.81; Volume Near Peak" *(New York Times),* 51
"Dr. Death." *see* Wojnilower, Albert M.
"Dr. Doom," 71, 81, 84
"Dr. Doom's Rally" *(Wall Street Journal),* 52
"Dr. Gloom," 93
Drew, Daniel, 136
Drysdale Government Securities, 133
Dun's Business Month, 128

E

East Asian financial markets, 12
econometrics, 147
economic and business forecasting
    by author, 80
    biases in, 146–149
    in *Blue Chip Report,* 77
    and COVID-19 pandemic (*see* new realities)
    criticisms of, 121
    future for, 151
    by Newton, 127

private-sector figures' influence in, 152

public-sector forecasting, 152

and reactions to negative predictions, 149

by Regan, 125

and structural change, 147–149

success at, 148–149

uncertainty in, 146

economic freedom, Hayek on, 66–67

economic health

in 1970s, 79–80, 82

and federal spending, 101–102

interest rates as indicator of, 5

post-COVID pandemic, 159–160

economic models, 146–147

economic stimulus packages, 144

Economist

on author and Reaganomics, 124

interview request from, 45

economy(-ies)

and COVID-19 crisis, 155 (*see also* new realities)

US (*see* US economy)

"The Education of David Stockman" (Greider), 126

Egypt–Israel Peace Treaty, 12

Empire State Building, 17

energy crisis, 80

Enron, 143

equities markets, 5. *see also* stock market(s)

equities research, 71, 79

"Euphoria on Wall Street" (*Washington Post*), 51

Euromoney, 127–128

Evansville Press, 122–123

exchange-traded funds, 159

Executive, 107

F

F5-E fighter jet (Asian Tiger), 12

family influences on author's views, 60

Fannie Mae, 143

fascism, Hayek on, 66

Federal Bureau of Investigation (FBI), 108

federal funds rate, 24, 142, 143

federal government. *see* US federal government

Federal Home Loan Bank Board, 13–14

Federal Open Market Committee, 140–142

Federal Reserve

Burns as chair of, 95

and Citibank's out-of-state deposit institution, 14

credit demand data from, 75

and dot-com boom and bust, 142

establishment of, 4

expected role of, 162

Federal Open Market Committee, 140–142

and growth of debt in 1970s, 83

Heller on, 68

and monetarism, 128

money supply increased by, 122

monitoring of, 74

Nadler at, 63

responses to COVID-19 crisis, 166, 169–170

role and effectiveness of, 155

and sale of Bear Stearns, 143

twenty-first-century policies of, 157–158

and understanding of structural changes, 148

Volcker's monetary policies at, 133–134

waning independence of, 166, 169

Federal Reserve Bank of New York, 67, 72, 94–96

Fed–Treasury Accord of March 1951, 166

fictional characterization of author, 114–115

Fidelity Savings and Loan Association of San Francisco, 13–14 finance, influences on author's thinking about. *see* intellectual roots of predicted change

"finance capitalism," age of, 3

"Financial Accounts of the United States," 75

financial assets, marketability of, 65

financial concentration, 148, 156–157, 161

financial crisis of 2008, 148, 169

financial deregulation
  in 1970s, 82–83
  in 1980s, 102

financial forecasting
  by author, 73
  biases in, 146–149
  and COVID-19 pandemic (*see* new realities)
  future for, 151
  private-sector figures' influence in, 152
  public-sector, 152
  and reactions to negative predictions, 149
  and social media, 164
  and structural change, 147–149
  success at, 148–149
  uncertainty in, 146

financial innovation
  in 1920s, 147–148
  in 1970s, 83

financial institutions. *see also* banks; investment firms/houses; Wall Street
  dynamic and static, 76
  financial concentration in, 148, 156–157, 161
  quasi-monopolistic role of, 157

"financialization" era, 4–5

financial markets. *see also* bond market; stock market; Wall Street
  in 1980s, 133
  during and after Great Recession, 145–147

creating flow data for, 76–78

in early 2020, 156

effect of government agency statements on, 152

expectations for Fed in, 169

global, author's effect on, 145

Homer on making forecasts of, 131–132

market dynamics in, 160–162

private-sector figures' influence on, 152

and Reaganomics, 124, 128

in second half of twentieth century, 137, 139

structural changes and behavior in, 148

in twenty-first century, 137–139

and US economy in 1970s, 80

financial sector, 3–4

"financial supermarkets," 13–14

"the Financial Supermarket" space, 25

financial system, Nadler's view of, 62

Financial Times, 44, 48–49

Financial Times industrial index, 31

Financial World Tonight, 45

First Boston Corporation, 96–97, 99

fiscalism, debate on monetarism versus, 67–69

fiscal policy
  in macroeconomic management, 67–69
  Nadler on, 64
  under Reagan, 123, 125, 126
  of Regan, 128

Fisk, "Jubilee Jim," 136

"Flow of Funds," 75

flow of funds analysis, 75–77, 83, 146

Foldessy, Ed, 36

Forbes, 124–125

Fortune, 36, 107

"the Foursome," 97–98

Freddie Mac, 143

Friedman, Milton, 67–69

Frinquelli, Michael, 87
futures market, author's influence on
    movements of, 129

G

"Gang of 6 Ambushing Reagan"
    (Newton), 126
Gardner, Charles, 44
Geithner, Timothy, 144
General Motors, 14
George Washington High School, 60, 61
Germany, 64, 67
Global Crossing, 143
Globe (Boston), 44
Golan Heights invasion, 13
Goldman Sachs, 143
gold standard, 148
Good Morning America, 45
Gould, Jay, 136
government(s). *see also* local governments;
    state governments; US federal
    government
        creditworthiness of, 169
        impact of COVID-19 crisis on, 165
        Smith on, 167
gradualism, 100–101
Grant, Jim, 36
Great Depression, 4, 148
Greenbaum, Mary, 36
Greenfield, Mary Ellen "Meg," 44
Greenspan, Alan, 2, 60, 140–142
Greider William, 126
Griggs, Bill, 97
Griggs & Santow Inc., 97
Gross Domestic Product (GDP), 76, 77
Gross National Product (GNP), 82
Gutfreund, John, 22–26
        author's relationship with, 85–86
        fining and resignation of, 154
        as managing partner, 85–86
        and Phibro-Salomon merger, 88, 89
        restructuring of firm by, 153–154
        and risk taking, 153

H

Habib, Philip, 12
Halsey Stuart, 97
*Handbook of Securities of the United
    States Government and Federal Agency
    Securities and Related Money Market
    Instruments,* 99
Hanner, Ken, 44
Harris, J. Ira, 18, 24
Hayek, Friedrich August von, 65–67
Heller, Walter, 67–69
Henry, John, 36
"Henry Kaufman" *(New York Times),* 49
"Henry Kaufman, America's Interest Rate
    Guru" *(Institutional Investor),* 107
"Henry Kaufman, Market Mover"
    (Wharton Account), 107
"Henry Who?" *(The Sydney Morning
    Herald),* 55
Herald Examiner (Los Angeles), 44
herding bias, 146
Hertzberg, Dan, 36
Hickman, W. Braddock "Brad," 147
historical data bias, 146–147
historical perspective on issues, 132–133
history, Nadler's view of, 62
A History of Interest Rates (Homer), 73
*A History of Interest Rates from 1000
    B.C. to the Present* (Homer), 132
Homer, Sidney, 72–78, 131–132, 145–146
Homer & Company, Inc., 73
Horowitz, Gedale, 22
household borrowing
        in 1920s, 148
        post-COVID pandemic, 159
        in recent years, 159
householders
        impact of COVID-19 crisis on, 165
        middle-class, 4
        near future financial position of, 159
        stock prices and interest rates
            monitored by, 2
House of Morgan, 3

"How Henry Kaufman Gets It Right" *(Fortune),* 107

"How Lovely to Be Famous" (New York Financial Writers Association), 110–111, 119

humorous depictions of author and forecasts, 109–119, 127

I

ImClone, 143

"In Binge of Optimism, Stock Market Surges By Record 38.81 Points" *(Wall Street Journal),* 50

independence, 154

industrial securities, emerging of market for, 3

"Industrials Rise Record 38.81 Points In Second-Heaviest Big Board Day" *(Wall Street Journal),* 50

inflation
    in 1970s, 80–82
    inability of governments to deal with, 80
    in post-World War II period, 7
    Volcker's approach to, 14, 83, 133–134

influences on author's views. *see* intellectual roots of predicted change

Information Revolution, 163–164

Inquirer, 44

Institutional Investor, 107, 111

insurance companies, 3, 87

intellectual roots of predicted change, 59–70
    debate on fiscalism versus monetarism, 67–69
    early childhood, 60
    education, 60–66
    Hayek, 65–67
    Homer, 73
    Nadler, 61–65

"Interest Plunges, Elevating Stocks to a Record Gain" *(New York Times),* 47

interest rate forecasts
    on August 17, 1982, 1, 8, 18–21, 24, 33–34, 104–105 *(see also* press reaction to prediction; public reaction to prediction)
    author's methodology for, 146
    and author's reputation, 80
    and business cycle, 80
    and flow of funds analysis, 75–77, 83, 146
    in late 1970s, 83
    market influence of, 122–123
    and Phibro-Salomon merger distractions, 90–91
    pressures on author concerning *(see* pressures concerning forecasts)
    and Regulation Q, 149
    of Wojnilower, 104

interest rates
    August 17, 1982 changes in, 29
    author's bearish stance on, 127, 128 *(see also* bearish views of author)
    on bonds, 134
    and business cycle, 80, 81
    changes in, following predicted decline, 29–32
    cyclical trends in, 132–133
    as economic performance indicator, 5
    federal funds rate, 24, 142
    Homer's history of, 132
    impact of COVID-19 crisis on, 166
    international, 13
    on long-term bonds, 5–7
    as major economic indicator and driver, 2–3
    and market gains, 140
    and monetarism, 67–69, 128
    monitoring of movements in, 2
    secular cycle in, 5–8, 81, 132–134, 145
    signals of, 7, 8
    stock prices, bond prices, and, 3
    and US economy in 1970s, 80

Volcker's approach to, 83
    Wojnilower on, 100, 103–104
international gold standard, 148
International Monetary Fund, 44
interview requests from press, 35–45
    decision to decline, 35–36
    on-air interviews, 45
    overseas press, 44–45
    US press, 36–43
investment banking
    in age of "finance capitalism," 3
    exit of Goldman Sachs and Morgan
        Stanley from, 143
    and financial conglomerate, 157, 158
    partnerships in, 87
    separation of commercial banking
        and, 97
investment banks, takeovers facilitated
    by, 158
investment firms/houses. see also Wall
    Street; individual firms
    bulge bracket of, 97
    research operations at, 71, 79
    shift from partnerships to
        corporations in, 153
investment grade corporate bonds, 158
investors, biases held by, 146
Ipsen, Eric, 36
Iversen, Torben, 66–67n

J

Johnson & Johnson, 158
Journal (Atlanta), 44
Journal of Commerce, 123, 125
JPMorgan Chase, 143

K

Katcher, Helen, 18, 23, 86
Kaufman, Elaine, 109, 129–130
"Kaufman of Salomon Bros." *(Executive),*
    107
Keynes, John Maynard, 67
Keynesianism, 67–69, 81

Kissinger Henry, 60
Korzeniowsky, Carol, 44
Kozma, Robert, 110
Kudlow, Lawrence, 126
Kuhn Loeb, 97

L

Lambert, Richard, 44
Langley, Bill, 44
Latin American debt crisis, 13–14
Leak, Tom, 36
Lehman Brothers, 143
Leigh, Richard, 44
Lenzner, Bob, 44–45
leveraged loan market, 159
Lewis, Michael, 28
Liar's Poker (Lewis), 28
"A Life in the Day of Henry Kaufman"
    (Nicol), 111, 113–114, 119
liquidity, 65, 160–162
local governments
    creditworthiness of, 169
    impact of COVID-19 crisis on, 165
London Daily Mail, 44
"A Long Trade Deficit" (Wojnilower), 103
Los Angeles Herald Examiner, 122
The Los Angeles Times (L.A. Times), 44,
    55, 122

M

macroeconomic policy debate, 67–69
Madden, John T., 64
Magnusson, Bob, 44
Malabre, Alfred, 73–74, 142–143
Manchester Guardian, 45
Manufacturers Hanover, 61
Manufacturers Hanover Trust, 29
market(s). see also financial markets; Wall
    Street
    and author's bullish position on
        bonds, 81
    author's influence on movements of,
        107–108, 121–123, 129, 150–152

bond (*see* bond market[s])
capital, 75
and concentration of power on Wall
     Street, 148
equities, 5
financial (*see* financial markets)
futures, 129
leveraged loan, 159
securities, from January 2008
     through March 2009, 143–144
stock (*see* stock market[s])
unregulated, 67
marketability, 65, 160–162
market making, 157
Martin, Doug, 36
Massachusetts Bank, 97
Mayer, Martin, 72, 75, 78, 143
McGowan, Wade, 129
McKeon, Jim, 76
media. *see also* press reaction to
   prediction; *individual media outlets*
     author quoted in, 78
     depictions of author in, 107, 109,
        111–119, 127–128
     and *Prospects for Financial Markets*
        publication, 78–79
     on Reaganomics, 124–127
Meet the Press, 77
"Megastar of Wall Street" *(Financial
   Times),* 48
Merrill Lynch, 31, 143, 152–153
Merrill Lynch, Pierce, Fenner & Smith, 74
Microsoft, 158
middle class, post-World War II, 4
Middle East peace negotiations, 12
military spending, 101–102, 123
Miller, G. William, 82, 95
monetarism, 67–69, 81, 128
monetary moderation policy, 157–158
monetary policy
     in *Comments on Credit,* 75
     and financial conglomerates, 157
     impact of COVID-19 crisis on, 166

monetary moderation, 157–158
Nadler on, 64
under Reagan, 123
of Volcker, 133–134
Money and Banking, 63
money management, 157
money supply, 67–69, 83, 122, 128
Morgan Stanley, 97, 143
Morgan Stanley Dean Witter, 140
mortgage-backed securities, 143
Mulally, Timothy, 11, 18
multinational corporations, 4
Munifacts News Wire, 36
Murdoch, Rupert, 108, 127

N

Nadler, Marcus, 61–65, 67
Nadler, Paul, 63, 64
Nasdaq, on March 15, 2000, 142
National Bureau of Economic Research,
   95
national debt, 14
     author's bearish stance on, 127
     current, 168
     in early 1980s, 101
     private borrowing crowded out by,
        124
     under Reaganomics, 123
National Socialism, 67
National Thrift News, 36
negative forecasts, 149
New Century, 143
New Deal, 97, 137
new housing activity, 133, 165
new realities, 155–170
     and corporate bonds, 158
     and financial concentration, 156–
        157, 161
     financial position of households, 159
     and Information Revolution, 163–
        164
     and market dynamics in financial
        markets, 160–162

and monetary moderation policy,
157–158
and political economy, 167–170
post-pandemic financing gap, 159–
160
and pre-COVID status quo, 155–164
and role of central banks, 162
and shadow banking system, 159
for the United States, 164–166
Newsweek, 36, 80
Newton, Maxwell, 108, 126–127
The New Yorker, 116
New York Financial Writers Association,
110–111, 119
The New York Post, 108, 118, 122,
126–127
New York Stock Exchange, 25n, 129
New York Times
on August 17, 1982, 11, 12
Baker's article in, 111, 112
on bond rally, 31
on Citibank, 14
on Friedman-Heller debate, 68, 69
on impact of author's prediction, 107
interview request from, 36
on July, 2002 bull markets, 142–143
on May 27, 1970 bull market, 138
on *Prospects for Financial Markets*
1982 findings, 122
on Reagan's tax increases, 15, 16
on results of August 17 prediction,
30, 47, 49, 51
on Wojnilower and interest rates,
104–105
Wojnilower's writings in, 101–103
New York University (NYU), University
Heights, 60, 61
New York University (NYU) Graduate
School of, 61–65, 68–69
Nicol, Eric, 111, 113–114, 119
Nightline, 45
Nightmare on Wall Street (Mayer), 143
Nikkei-Dow Jones, 31

NN Corp., 87
noise, 7
Northrop Corporation, 12

O

Obama, Barack, 144
The Observer (London), 44
Olesky, Jon, 142
O'Neill, Thomas P. "Tip," 125
One New York Plaza, 25
On Money and Markets(Kaufman), 60,
100n
optimism, 149

P

Palestine Liberation Organization, 12
Paulson, Henry "Hank," Jr., 144
Paulus, John D., 16
PBS, 45
Penn Square, 133
People's Industrial Bank, 61
Perlmutter, Tom, 36
Phibro Corporation, 23, 86–91
Phibro-Salomon, 23, 87–91, 154
The Philadelphia Inquirer, 53
"Pink Book," 99
political economy(-ies)
collectivist, 66
impact of COVID-19 crisis on,
167–170
political freedom, Hayek on, 66–67
"Poor Henry Kaufman" *(Institutional
Investor),* 111
Pope, Alexander, 85
"Portfolio Managers to Henry K.: 'You're
Wrong.'" *(Bondweek),* 127
Power, Jerome, 170
press reaction to prediction, 35–55. *see
also* public reaction to prediction
declining of interview requests, 35–36
interview requests from US press,
37–43
on-air interview requests, 45

overseas requests for interviews,
44–45
representative sample of, 46–55
pressures concerning forecasts, 121–134
and author's market movement
influence, 122–123
and early August bond market rally,
130–131
and economic developments, 133–
134
and historical perspective on issues,
132–133
press coverage, 122–129
and Reaganomics, 121, 123–127
and unpopularity of bearish stance,
127–129
private equity funds, 159
productivity
in 1970s US economy, 79
in 1980s US economy, 133
Prospects for Financial Markets, 75–78,
83–84, 122, 125, 151
public reaction to prediction, 107–119
criticisms, 108
fictional characterization, 114–115
humorous, 109–119
positive articles, 107
by press, 107, 109, 111–119 (*see also*
press reaction to prediction)
threats, 108–109
public-sector forecasting, 152

Q
Quint, Mike, 36

R
Raines, Howell, 15, 16
Rand, Ayn, 66
Reagan, Ronald
on deficit reduction, 46
deregulation under, 102
economic program of (*see*
Reaganomics)

and monetary policy, 123
promises of administration of, 84
supply-side approach of, 14–15
taxes raised by, 15, 16
Reaganomics, 126
administration's shifting view of,
125–126
criticisms for going against, 93n
and pressure on author concerning
forecasts, 121, 123–127
reliance on monetarism in, 128
supporters of, 107, 108
taxes under, 123, 125, 126, 129
"Reagan Recession," 14
Record (Hackensack, New Jersey), 44
Regan, Donald, 125
Regulation Q, 82–83, 149
research operations
and current realities on Wall Street,
153
at Federal Reserve Bank of New
York, 94–95
Gutfreund's attitude toward, 85–86
and incorporation of Wall Street, 154
at investment houses, 71, 79
and Phibro-Salomon merger, 90–91
and respect for boundaries, 152
at Salomon Brothers, 71, 73, 78–79,
145–146, 151
residential investments, in 1970s, 82
Reuters, 36
risk, 149, 153
The Road to Financial Reformation
(Kaufman), 102n
The Road to Serfdom (Hayek), 66
"The Room," 25–28
Roosa, Robert, 94
Roosevelt, Franklin, 137
Rosenthal, Richard, 18, 88
Russia, debt default by, 141
Rutberg, Sidney, 113–114

S

Sadat, Anwar, 12

Safety Fund Bank, 97

Salomon, William R. "Billy," 22–23, 150
  on author as first "Fed watcher," 72
  and author's appointment to
    Executive Committee, 78
  and author's relationship with
    Gutfreund, 86
  and Homer's recruitment, 73
  as managing partner, 85
  and Phibro-Salomon merger, 89–90
  research operations support from,
    151

Salomon Brothers
  author as "Fed watcher" at, 65, 72,
    73
  author as figurehead for work of, 59
  author's accomplishments at, 145–
    146
  author's prominence at, 71, 78
  author's resignation from, 153–154
  author's years at, 67, 73
  Bond Market Review, 74
  Bond Market Roundup, 74, 130, 131
  Comments on Credit, 75
  demise of, 154
  in early 1980s, 85
  Executive Committee of, 78, 89–90,
    145, 153–154
  Friedman-Heller debate funded by,
    68–69
  growth and reputation of, 59
  Gutfreund as managing partner at,
    85–86
  Gutfreund's restructuring of, 153–
    154
  Homer recruited by, 73
  Hong Kong office of, 12
  incorporation of, 86, 153
  integration of activities at, 25–26
  Kaufman's interest rates prediction
    for, 19–21, 33–34

Office of the Chairman at, 153–154
  at One New York Plaza, 25
  Phibro Corporation merger with, 23,
    87–91
  and presentations of *Prospects for*
    Financial Markets report, 78
  Prospects for Financial Markets,
    75–78, 83–84, 122, 125, 151
  research operation at, 71, 73, 78–79,
    145–146, 151
  and threats against author, 108–109
  "tigers" offerings of, 31
  trading floor of, 25–28
  as world's leading bond trader, 1

Salomon Brothers Executive Committee
  meeting (August 17,1982), 11, 17–25
  author's representation of interests
    in, 59
  interruption of, 23–25
  participants in, 18, 22–23
  prediction of interest rates presented
    at, 18–21, 24

Samuelson, Paul, 2

Santow, Leonard J., 97

satires about author and forecasts, 127–
  128

Schmeelk, Richard "Mr. Canada," 18,
  22, 89

Schumpeter, Joseph, 163

Scudder, Stevens & Clark, 73

secular cycle for interest rates, 5–8, 81,
  132–134, 145

securities markets, from January 2008
  through March 2009, 143–144

securities trading, 87–88, 161

"Seer Talks, Dow Listens" *(The Los*
  Angeles Times), 55

"Seventh Annual Arthur K. Salomon
  Lecture," 68–69

shadow banking system, 159

"shiftability" theory of commercial
  banking, 65

Shilling, A. Gary, 73–74, 152–153

Sicilia, David, 140–141
Sigma Photo News, 44
signals, 7, 8
Simon, Charles "Charlie," 73, 78
Sinai Peninsula invasion, 12–13
Smith, Adam, 167–168
social welfare spending, under Reagan, 123
Solow, Robert, 124
Someone Else's Money (Thomas), 114–115
Soskice, David, 66–67n
speculation, 148, 158
"Stabilize Banking" (Wojnilower), 102–103
Stahl, David, 36
Standard & Poor's (S&P) Index, 29, 31, 139
state governments
    creditworthiness of, 169
    impact of COVID-19 crisis on, 165
statism, 167, 168, 170
Stock, Craig, 44
Stockman, David, 125–126
stock market(s). *see also* financial markets
    1920s speculation in, 148
    1945–2019, 138–144
    after modified stance on interest rates, 123
    after *Prospects for Financial Markets* 1982 findings, 122
    on August 17, 1982, 1
    author's influence on movements of, 129
    crash of 1929, 137
    effect of interest rate prediction on, 25
    in Gilded Age, 137
    major movements in, 2
    trades on August 17, 1982, 29–30
    in twentieth century, 137
"Stock Market Records Its Largest Jump Ever" *(New York Times),* 51

stock prices
    bond prices, interest rates, and, 3
    and dot-com bubble, 141
    monitoring of movements in, 2
Strauss, Thomas, 22, 24
structural change, 147–149
subprime mortgage crisis (2007–2009), 138
subprime mortgages, 143
success, overestimating likelihood of, 149
Sullivan, Brian, 44
Sunday New York Times, 80
supply-side approach, 14–15, 121, 124–125
The Sydney Morning Herald, 55
synthetic derivatives, 143

T

Taiwan, F5-E fighter jet manufacturing agreement with, 12
Tarnowsky, Tom, 36
taxes, under Reagan, 15, 123, 125, 126, 129
technology, 163, 164
Tectonic Shifts (Kaufman), 82n
Tendler, David, 23, 86–87
Thomas, Michael M., 114–115
threats, following August 17 prediction, 108–109
Time magazine, 36, 93
Times Herald (Dallas), 44
Time Warner, 158
trade deficit, Wojnilower on, 103
Travelers Group, 154
Tribune (Chicago), 44

U

uncertainty
    about financial assets' marketability, 65
    in economic and financial forecasting, 146
    mid-1982 atmosphere of, 12

"Undercover Socialists of America"
(Newton), 125
unemployment rate, 14
in 1980s, 133
in early 2020, 156
impact of COVID-19 crisis on, 165
unregulated markets and currencies, 67
UPI, 36
U.S. News & World Report, 128–129
US Council of Economic Advisers, 95
US dollar, 168, 169
US economy
in 1970s, 79–82
in 1980s, 133
and COVID-19 crisis, 155
in early 1980s, 102, 133
US federal government
budget deficit of, 14–15, 101–102
(*see also* national debt)
impact of COVID-19 crisis on,
165–166
and post-pandemic financing gap,
159–160
post-World War II investments of, 4
prevented bankruptcies of, 3
state and local governments'
dependence on, 169
World War II restructuring of finance
during, 148
US government bonds
and author's bullish position, 81
overseas investors' preference for, 169
post-World War II period yield on, 7
predicted fall in interest rates for, 24
yield on, in 1970s, 80
US Treasury, 74, 169
US Treasury bills, 16, 80, 133
US Treasury bonds, 26, 29

V

Vartan, Vartanig G., 99
Volcker, Paul, 15
author's relationship with, 94

in "the Foursome" lunch club, 97
in "Gang of 6 Ambushing Reagan,"
126
and inflation, 14
inflation measures of, 83
and monetarist policy, 128
results of policies of, 7
Vouté, William, 18

W

wages
in 1970s US economy, 79
downward pressure on, 163–164
Waldorf-Astoria Hotel, 16–18
"Wall St. gains record 38.81" *(Financial
Times),* 49
Wall Street. *see also* financial markets;
investment firms/houses
and author's influence over market
movements, 107–108
concentration of power on, 148
current realities on, 153
and independence of research
function, 154
investment banking partnerships on,
87
October volatility on, 140
in postwar period, 137
Reaganomics position of, 125
record days on, 137–144
risk-taking culture of, 145
structural changes on, 83
Wall Street Crash of 1929, 4
Wall Street Journal
on August 17, 1982, 11, 12
on author's forecasts, 122
on interest rates, 16
interview request from, 36, 44
on March 15, 2000 bull market,
141–142
on October 20, 1987 bull market,
138

quoting Wojnilower on interest rates,
104
on result of author's August 17
prediction, 47, 50, 52
on September 8, 1998, FOMC
meeting, 141
"Wall Street seer surprises his fans
with bullish turn" *(The Philadelphia
Inquirer)*, 53
Wall Street Week with Louis Rukeyser,
45, 77
"Wall St surge as Kaufman predicts
interest rate fall" *(Financial Times)*, 48
Walter E. Heller International, 18
Wanniski, Jude, 126
Washington Mutual, 143
Washington Post, 44, 51, 122
Washington Times, 44
weak debt, 163
"wealth effect," 2
The Wealth of Nations (Smith), 167–168
Weidenbaum, Murray L., 125
Wenings, Germany, 60, 86
Wharton Account, 107
"When Henry Speaks..." *(Courier
Express)*, 52
"Wild times on Wall Street" *(Financial
Times)*, 49

"The Wizard of Wall Street" *(New York
Times)*, 107
Wojnilower, Albert M. "Dr. Death,"
93–105
August 16, 1982 memo of, 46,
103–104
author's relationship with, 94, 98
career of, 94–100
early life of, 94
education of, 94, 95
forecasts of, 93
in "Gang of 6 Ambushing Reagan,"
126
on interest rates, 16, 46, 100, 103–
104
luncheon club organized by, 97–98
public profile of, 99–100
reputation of, 93–94
on today's Fed, 162
in "Undercover Socialists of
America," 125
writings of, 98–103
Wolfe, Tom, 26–27
Wriston, Walter, 13

Y

Yahoo!, 141
Yellen, Janet, 170

ABOUT THE AUTHOR

Henry Kaufman is President of Henry Kaufman & Company, Inc., a firm established in April 1988 specializing in economic and financial consulting and now a family investment office. For the previous twenty-six years, he was with Salomon Brothers Inc., where he was a Senior Partner, Managing Director, Member of the Executive Committee, and head of the firm's four research departments. He was also a Vice Chairman of the parent company, Salomon Inc. Before joining Salomon Brothers, Dr. Kaufman was in commercial banking and served as an economist at the Federal Reserve Bank of New York.

Born in Germany in 1927, Kaufman received a BA in economics from New York University in 1948, an MS in finance from Columbia University in 1949, and a PhD in banking and finance from the New York University Graduate School of Business Administration in 1958. He also received an honorary Doctor of Laws degree from New York University in 1982, and honorary Doctor of Humane Letters degrees from Yeshiva University in 1986 and from Trinity College in 2005.

Over his long, distinguished Wall Street career, Dr. Kaufman has met with central bankers and other leaders in business and government around the world, and delivered scores of addresses at prominent organizations in finance, economics, and business.

He is author of hundreds of essays and editorials in the *New York Times*, *Wall Street Journal*, *Financial Times*, *Fortune* magazine, *Business Week*, and other leading periodicals as well as four previous books: *Interest Rates, the Markets, and the New Financial World* (which was awarded the first George S. Eccles Prize for excellence in economic writing from the Columbia Business School); *On Money and Markets: A Wall Street Memoir*; *The Road to Financial Reformation: Warnings, Consequences, Reforms*; and *Tectonic Shifts in Financial Markets: People, Policies, and Institutions.*

In addition to his business activities, Dr. Kaufman has been active in a number of public organizations including as a Member of the Board of Trustees and Chairman Emeritus at the Institute of International Education; Member of the Board of Trustees and Member of the Investment Committee, Norton Museum of Art; Member and Chairman Emeritus of the Board of Overseers, Stern School of Business, New York University; Member of the Board of Governors, Tel Aviv University; Fellow, American Academy of Arts & Sciences; Former Treasurer, The Economic Club of New York; Honorary Trustee and Former President, The Animal Medical Center; Life Trustee, New York University; and Life Trustee, The Jewish Museum. He has been a major benefactor of the Institute of International Education; New York University, through the Kaufman Management Center; and the Kaufman Music Center in New York City; and has endowed professorships in financial and business history at five universities.

Henry Kaufman lives in Franklin Lakes, New Jersey, and Palm Beach, Florida, with his wife, Elaine. They have three sons—Craig, Daniel, and Glenn.